Ablaze

STORIES OF
DARING
TEEN SAINTS

Colleen Swaim

Liguori
LIGUORI, MISSOURI

Imprimi Potest: Harry Grile, CSsR
Provincial, Denver Province, The Redemptorists
Published by Liguori Publications, Liguori, Missouri 63057
To order, call 800-325-9521 or visit liguori.org

Library of Congress Cataloging-in-Publication Data

Swaim, Colleen.
    Ablaze : stories of daring teen saints / Colleen Swaim.—1st ed.
        p. cm.
    ISBN 978-0-7648-2029-8
    1. Christian saints—Biography. 2. Catholic teenagers—Religious life. I. Title. II. Title:
Stories of daring teen saints.
    BX4655.3.S93 2011
    282.092'2—dc22
    [B]
                            2011009120

Printed in the United States of America
15 14 13 12 11   /   5 4 3 2

First edition

Contents

Dedication

In memory of my grandfather, William L. Johncox (1923-2010), who introduced the teenage me to T.S. Eliot, and whose creative humor, legal mind, and zeal for all things Ohio continue to impact.

Acknowledgments

This book would not have my name on it were it not for my husband, Matt Swaim, who passed the project into my in box. Thank you for subscribing to the notion that I should take it on even before I did, giving publishing advice and encouragement in the face of looming deadlines, and taking up the household chore slack. I would have been wearing some pretty dirty socks for a couple of months if it hadn't been for you, my very own Innocent Smith.

To my parents and first catechists, Doug and Kris Johncox, who somehow helped me survive high school, even though I wasn't nearly a saint. To Patty Kues, for introducing me to matoke, and to Rita Heikenfeld, for the use of her incredible chai recipe.

To those people I've never met in the flesh who aided me tremendously in the formation of this book, especially Dr. Matthew Bunson, through whom I first learned, via Matt, of Blessed Chiara Luce, and Reverend Jose R. Arong, who sent this total stranger his own reading material on Blessed Pedro Calungsod. To Father Ted Ross, whose infectious Jesuit history knowledge led my husband to become fascinated with Saint Stanislaus and spread the contagion on to me.

To my students at Newport Central Catholic High School, for their interest in this project, perspectives on what it should encompass, and reminders that being a modern-day teenager is far from uncomplicated. Strive with all your might for sanctity.

And lastly, to Saint Alphonsa, Blessed Chiara, Saint Dominic, Saint Kizito, Saint Maria, Blessed Pedro, Saint Stanislaus and Saint Teresa, whose intercessions have become tremendous parts of my life. Your heroic virtues at such tender ages galvanize me to get it together. I can't wait to meet you.

Introduction

"If you are what you should be,
you will set the whole world ablaze!"

—Pope John Paul II,
paraphrasing Saint Catherine of Siena, World Youth Day 2000

We live in a world that scoffs at the foolishness of saints—those remarkable people who look beyond their own reality to that paradise set aside for us by the infinite Creator. The people profiled in this book are not the stuff of fairy tales or robots, but, amazingly, flesh-and-blood teenagers who lived in the midst of temptation and adverse world views and who did what many people twice their age cannot bring themselves to do, which is to live radically on fire for Christ. While the current age holds a new level of accessible moral dilemmas for its young people, the saints and blesseds within these pages dealt with a good deal of the same struggles and consequently serve as models of right living beyond the confines of their own times.

As we see in Ecclesiastes 1:9–10, "What has been, that will be; what has been done, that will be done. Nothing is new under the sun. Even the thing of which we say, 'See, this is new!' has already existed in the ages that preceded us," and so it is true of these holy ones and the daring trails they blazed—those same paths are still open more than ever to us. And so I invite you to come on a journey across time and land masses and learn a little bit about your own very real potential for true holiness, because we are all called to become ablaze with the boldness of the saints.

HOW TO USE THIS BOOK

You'll notice when you start to turn these pages that *Ablaze* isn't your ordinary stories-of-the-saints book. I've filled these pages with tons of extras that will bring these eight zealous young Christians to life and will inspire you to live out your faith with their same fire. The main focus of each chapter is the story of the particular saint, but as you'll see, there is so much more.

Since our Catholic faith has been practiced in so many different ways, and because the teens featured here come from a variety of times and places, you'll find info and important definitions in the boxes scattered throughout the text. Read up—you just might learn something!

To help you apply what you're reading to your own life, I've included reflection questions throughout each story to think and journal about. Journaling pages can be found at the end of each chapter.

You will also find Scripture verses, pictures, quotes, and other fun tidbits scattered throughout the stories. Take them in, write them down, think about them for awhile—they are all meant to bring the saint to life and inspire you with their holiness!

At the end of each story is a prayer, usually one that the person you've just read about said or wrote. Take a moment while you're in a thoughtful mode and inspired by these saintly stories to pray. We know that these men and women are powerful intercessors with God.

Finally, you'll find "Saintly Challenges" at the end of each chapter. These are ideas of things you can do to connect even deeper with the life of the person you've just read about. I've included everything from movie nights to journaling questions to recipes—there really is something for everyone, so dig in.

At the end of the book are some additional materials that can help you delve into the teachings from the *Catechism of the Catholic Church* that connect to the stories in this book. Remember to check them out!

SAINT DOMINIC SAVIO

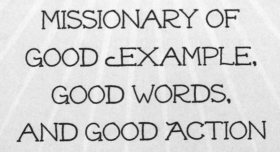

MISSIONARY OF
GOOD EXAMPLE,
GOOD WORDS,
AND GOOD ACTION

"Like Saint Dominic Savio,
be missionaries of good example, good words,
good action at home, with neighbors,
and colleagues at work. At every age we can and
we must bear witness to Christ! Commitment to
bear witness is permanent and daily."

POPE JOHN PAUL II, DECEMBER 7, 1997, HOMILY

FEAST DAY: MARCH 9

PATRONAGES: THOSE FALSELY ACCUSED, CHOIRBOYS

Dominic was born on April 2, 1842, to Charles and Brigid Savio, growing up outside of Turin, Italy. Dominic's father was a blacksmith, and with ten children, they didn't have a lot of money. According to his parents, Dominic was a loving and obedient son from his early years. In fact, by age four, he was even saying his morning and bedtime prayers himself. This young child, who attended and served daily Mass by the age of five, prayed the Angelus and would even remind his family to say grace before meals. If the door to church was locked when he got there, he knelt on the ground until it was opened, even if it was snowy or dirty, and would cheerfully wave at the priest when they would meet on the street. When he was a little older, he would go out of his way to help his father with chores.

> **Angelus:** A prayer said in celebration of God being made flesh in the person of Christ Jesus, including Mary's role in the event through her "Yes" to becoming his mother.

As a little kid, how did you live out your faith? How has that changed as you've grown older?

As Dominic grew, so did his strong faith. He consistently went to confession, even as a young child, and was permitted to receive his first Communion early, because he understood the Real Presence of the Eucharist ahead of the other children. In order to prepare himself for the sacrament, the night before his first Communion Dominic asked his mother for forgiveness for anything he had done to disappoint or hurt her, and promised not to do so again. He was genuinely sorry, cried, and was first to arrive at the church the next morning. When he made his first Communion in 1849, he made several promises, such as, "I will go to confession, and I will go to holy Communion as often as I am allowed, I will try to give Sundays and holy days completely to God, my best friends will be Jesus and Mary, and Death, but not sin." These would prove to be more than just words, but a living pledge that he kept until the end of his life.

At age ten, Dominic finished at the village school and started at the county school three miles away. Savio means "wise," and Dominic did his best to live up to it at school. He was disciplined about working to do well at school and avoided trouble-makers' attempts to get him to join them in their mischief. He even attempted to help those who were struggling and to reform those who misbehaved, sometimes earning him the disdain of his classmates.

Dominic was not a strong boy but was known by his teachers, schoolmates, and even his principal as a cheerful and pleasant young man. Even with his health problems, Dominic never missed a day of school. A hard worker, Dominic rose to the top of his class and was always ready to help those who weren't as interested in their studies. His principal observed that Dominic excelled "not simply because he was clever but because he worked very hard and came to have a great love for his lessons. It was also because his studies were not simply for himself but for God."

What motivates you to try to do well academically?

His life at school was not without challenges. One day his schoolmates blamed Dominic for cramming the classroom's stove with trash and snow. Strangely, he did nothing to defend himself. It was not until the next day, when the truth was revealed, that the principal, Father Cugliero, realized Dominic had not been involved. When asked why he did not claim his innocence, Dominic explained that he knew the boys who had done it would be expelled for what they had done, and he wanted to spare their punishment. "I remembered that Jesus had been blamed unjustly and had not said anything," Dominic said, "and I thought I should do the same." It was a truly selfless act that made a lasting impact on his principal, and would later make Dominic the patron saint of those falsely accused.

In 1854, Father Cugliero went to see Saint John Bosco about admitting Dominic to his school, the Oratory of Saint Francis de Sales. Attesting to Dominic's high standing in his school, both for his character and for his academics, Father Cugliero claimed, "You may have in your house boys equally good and clever, but there are none better than him." When he introduced himself to Father Bosco, Dominic told him that he'd like to be a priest. As a test of his academic skill, Bosco had him read and memorize a page of the Mass readings, intending for him to work on it overnight. Don Bosco was astounded when Dominic had memorized and could explain it within ten minutes, and he immediately decided that Dominic would attend the oratory. Joyfully, Dominic promised Don Bosco "...always to act in such a way that you will never have reason to complain of me," and accompanied him to Turin, where he would begin studies.

Dominic continued to follow the rules at school and was a good student in the classics. He sought the normal life of a student, even asking one of the teachers for guidance on how to make the best of his experience there. Others, whether they were devout or not, liked spending time with him, as he told amusing stories, enjoyed playing games, and avoided complaining and finding fault with things. He especially sought out boys who had no one else to be their friend, as well as those who were sick. Dominic enjoyed the normal life of a student, with all of its ups and downs, if not with a few

The classics: The study of ancient Greek and Latin people and languages, as well their civilizations, was very popular when Saint Dominic was a teenager.

saintly exceptions. In the midst of playing sports, he would sometimes ask his companions to come to confession with him later on.
Occasionally Dominic would even withdraw from them to behold
heavenly visions.

*Would you have the courage to invite a friend to come along with you to
church? Why or why not?*

He hadn't been in the oratory long before Dominic decided that
he wanted to become a saint. He wanted "...to give up everything
to Jesus and for always. If I am not trying to be a saint, I am doing
nothing at all. I will not have any peace if I don't keep on trying." He
appealed to Father Bosco for guidance. It was suggested to Dominic
that one key action of a saint might be to bring others to know God,
which pleased him greatly as he thought of how thrilled he would
be "...if only I could win all my companions for God."

*Everyone is called to be a saint. Have you been living like it's only for a
select, VIP crowd, or have you taken on the challenge as your own? How
has this affected the way you live as a Catholic teenager?*

Dominic's favorite saints were those who had worked in the
missions, living for the purpose of winning souls for Christ. Had he
known of him, he surely would have admired the efforts of Blessed
Pedro Calungsod, who went so far as to give his life for the sake of
missionary zeal, but as Dominic didn't have funds to send to the missions he instead kept them in prayer, offering his reception of Communion for them once a week. Volunteering as a religious educator,
both in Sunday School and privately, Dominic brought his missionary spirit to the oratory, even though he sometimes was made fun
of by other boys for his labors.

Even with his saintly character, Dominic faced the same challenges of peer pressure that many young people do today. One day Dominic almost skipped school with a group of other boys in order to go the fair. But before they missed any of their classes, Dominic came to his senses and decided to go to school. He even chastised the other boys, telling them, "If we stay away we are displeasing God and also our superiors." With that, Dominic had swayed the crowd, and the other boys were convinced that they should head to class, too.

On another occasion, Dominic heard there was to be a fight between two older students and tried to talk them down from violence. When they refused, Dominic asked the boys if he could set the conditions for their fight. The boys agreed they'd go along with Dominic's plan, just as long as he wouldn't keep them from fighting. He led them out and seemed to be setting up an arena as a site for their fight. Then Dominic stopped and pulled out the crucifix from around his neck, and, holding it up, said courageously, "I want each of you to look at this crucifix and throw a stone at me, saying clearly these words: 'Jesus Christ, who was innocent, died forgiving his enemies; I, a sinner, am going to offend him by this deliberate act of revenge.'" He then went to each boy, telling him to throw a stone at him. Neither boy did. Dominic had won: there would be no fight. It was the would-be stone throwers themselves who went and told others about Dominic's role in this incident.

Recall a time when you did your best to help a friend or friends avoid a bad call.

Dominic's faith grew while he was at the oratory. There, he was encouraged to go often to the sacraments of confession and holy Communion, and to choose a priestly confessor who could offer him consistent spiritual guidance. Dominic gradually began becoming more active in his already-flourishing sacramental life and would go to confession each week and would receive the Eucharist every day. Dominic made sure he was spiritually prepared before receiving Communion and even dedicated his reception of Communion every day of the week to a different prayer intention. His attraction to the Eucharist was so strong that he could lose track of time when praying in front of the Blessed Sacrament and someone would have to go find him when he was needed elsewhere.

How do you prepare yourself to receive Jesus' body, blood, soul, and divinity in the Eucharist?

Through the struggles of his youth, Dominic gained a firm belief in the restorative power of confession. He approached his confessor as "the doctor of the soul," and sought his advice—and the medicine of God's grace—often. "I have full confidence in my confessor, who is so kind and helpful to me," Dominic said, "and I don't think I have any trouble that he cannot cure." And Dominic was right—his confessor does seem to have guided the young man's spirit toward Christ. Dominic tried to go to confession as much as three times a week, but his spiritual director wisely disagreed that this was a good idea, as he rightly believed the young man dealt with the spiritual struggle of scruples. Instead, he advised him to deal admirably with the little difficulties of life, rather than seeking out the more outwardly impressive penance of fasting, by offering to Jesus his daily struggles.

> **Scruples:** An unfounded apprehension and consequently unwarranted fear that something is a sin when it is not.

Dominic diligently followed his confessor's advice to take up little, everyday crosses. Realizing that the tongue can do serious damage, he strove to not cut people off when they were speaking, or to take over conversations. He likewise did his best not to waste food, believing that, "Everything that we have is God's precious gift."

8

Ablaze

He also cheerfully did the most menial of tasks for the greater glory of God. In all of these seemingly small acts, Dominic continued his path to holiness.

Prayer played an important part in Dominic's life at the oratory. He tried to spend quiet time with spiritual readings or talking to God, and he had a special love for Mary. In 1854, the dogma of the Immaculate Conception was defined, and on the feast's vigil, Dominic prayed with conviction, "Mary, I give you my heart, please keep it always as your own. Jesus and Mary, always be my friends." In honor of Mary, he prayed at the altar dedicated to the Immaculate Heart of Mary; partook in May devotions dedicated to Our Lady, such as doing a special action in her recognition every day; and he even raffled off his own book in order to put in for

Immaculate Conception: When you think of the phrase "Immaculate Conception," it's common to think of Jesus, who was conceived by the power of the Holy Spirit and born to Mary, his mother, but actually it refers Mary, who was herself conceived without sin in the womb of her mother and born to Anne and Joachim. The feast of the Immaculate Conception is celebrated on December 8.

the costs of a Marian altar for his dorm at school. He and his friends founded a Sodality of Mary Immaculate in her honor, and together promised to receive Communion regularly, follow the school's rules, and to help each other in their pursuits of holiness.

The Immaculate Heart of Mary

Especially in light of his devotion to Mary, Dominic tried to be conscious of how he looked at girls. Dominic saw that his struggle to look at others purely was part of growing up, but he did not make excuses when it was difficult. "The eyes are two windows," he said, "Through these windows what you let pass, passes. You can let an angel in or you can let the devil in, and whichever you let in can get possession of your heart." To assume that guarding his heart was an easy task for such a holy teenager would be wrong, as Dominic himself admitted. Sometimes he would get a violent headache as he struggled to control his eyes and heart. The effort was good practice for when Dominic would have to put his morals into action in other situations. For instance, one day a boy brought a pornographic magazine to school. Dominic grabbed it from him and tore it up, reproaching his classmate. "God has given us our eyes to admire the wonders of creation," Dominic reminded him. "You know well enough that one look is enough to stain your soul, and yet you go feasting your eyes on this." This type of response would have been a lot more difficult for Dominic had he not been living chastely on a daily basis already.

Do you have the strength to do as Dominic did and stand up to class-mates, teammates, or friends who are misusing the gifts of the senses? How can you live chastely in a world that makes it easy to do otherwise?

Dominic was always known to be weak of health. At the time, the doctors couldn't pinpoint exactly what was wrong with him and diagnosed no specific disease, instead only saying that he was of "delicate constitution." The only way to preserve his life would have been to send him away from school to a quiet life at home, where he could do small tasks that would not tax his mind or his body. In fact, the doctor recommended that "...the best remedy would be to let him go to heaven: he seems to me to be very ready for it." And so rather than taking to a sick bed, Dominic's life continued as usual.

So while his parents, doctors, and teachers would urge special care of him, Dominic would always push himself. He did not want to leave his friends and studies at the oratory. Even though he had long been sick at school, Dominic was so uncomplaining and typically in a good mood that his schoolmates assumed that he had been much healthier than he actually was. As he didn't have to stay in bed, he went to class and enjoyed helping in the school's sick area.

Eventually, Dominic's weakening health led him to be sent home from the oratory, though he soon returned and was sent home once again. Don Bosco asked why he was unwilling to go home and stay there with his parents, and Dominic simply replied that he wanted to spend the rest of his life at the oratory. "I know that if I go home, I shall never come back," he said. All in all, Dominic had spent three years at the oratory, and so it was on March 1, 1857, at 2 p.m., that he left the oratory in Turin one last time.

His health seemed to improve back at home, until his family started to realize that a cough was getting worse and he wasn't eating enough. The doctor took Dominic's condition seriously, and he was ordered to stay in bed and rest. Later, the doctor believed that Dominic was suffering from inflammation and prescribed a course of ten bleedings. Dominic cheerfully responded to his illness and to the painful treatment, and he didn't whine over the bleedings or the nasty medicine, keeping it all in a prayerful perspective. "What is this," he said, "compared with the piercing of Jesus' hands and feet with the nails?"

Bleedings: A common medical practice during Dominic's time and long before. Bloodletting, many times achieved by attaching leeches to the skin, was thought by many doctors to be a practical cure-all.

Think back to the last time you were in physical pain. How did you react to it?

While his doctor and parents were confident that he was improving, Dominic knew his illness was more serious and took time to prepare himself for death. He asked his dad to "give the heavenly doctor a chance," and asked to receive the sacraments of confession and holy Communion. A priest came at once. "Now I am happy," Dominic said. "I have a long journey to eternity, but with Jesus by my side I fear nothing. How I wish I could say it to the whole world, when Jesus is with us there is no fear of anything—not even of death itself." It is plain that Dominic's response to his illness wasn't the average, as he faced his own death with courage.

By March 9, 1857, the doctor and Dominic's family were again sure that he would get better. While he sounded strong, he was constantly indicating to his family and friends that he didn't believe he had much time left. Dominic asked that the priest come and give him the sacrament of the anointing of the sick. Before the anointing, Dominic prayed, "Dear Jesus, I love you and I wish to love you for all eternity—forgive me my sins. Let this sacrament wipe out all the sins I have ever committed by my eyes, my ears, my lips, and my feet: may my soul and body be made holy by the merits of your sacred passion. Amen."

The priest advised Dominic to think about Christ's passion as he faced the last hours of his illness. The teenager slept for half an hour before waking to ask, "Dad, are you there?" His father stayed by his side, reading him prayers from the Exercise of a Happy Death. After responding to the prayers, Dominic fell in and out of sleep until finally saying, "Goodbye, Dad, goodbye...What was it the parish priest suggested to me...I don't seem to remember...Oh, what wonderful things I see..."

He then died with a smile on his face and was so peaceful that his father thought that he was asleep; he was one month from turning fifteen. From the time Dominic died, his friends and family believed him to be a saint. A month after Dominic's death, his father had a vision wherein Dominic consoled him, assuring, "...I really am in heaven."

PRAYER OF SAINT DOMINIC SAVIO

O Jesus, my liberty I give completely to you:
My body with all its powers I give completely to you.
Everything I have is yours, O God,
And I abandon myself completely to your holy will.
Amen.

MEMORY VERSE
ROMANS 6:9

We know that Christ, raised from the dead,
dies no more; death no longer has power over him.

Do you think death had power over Saint Dominic? Explain.

Do you have fears regarding death? If so, what are they?

Saintly Challenges

- Dominic means "of the Lord" and Savio means "wise." Do a little investigating to find out what your own name means.

- When he started at the oratory, Dominic conferred with a teacher with an aim at understanding everything that was expected of him at his new school. Review the general rules or student handbook of your own school. Which rules are you keeping? Which could you use a little brushing up on?

- We know from Saint John Bosco, Dominic's teacher and mentor, that Dominic wore a crucifix. Make an effort to wear one in order to remind yourself of Christ's victory over sin through his saving death on the cross.

- Today, do your best to, like Dominic, really listen to the other person in a conversation, striving to not cut him or her off or monopolize the discussion.

JOURNAL YOUR THOUGHTS

JOURNAL YOUR THOUGHTS

SAINT TERESA OF THE ANDES

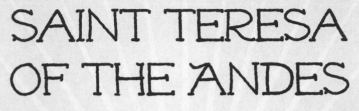

PURE BEAUTY AND HAPPINESS

"The young virgin of the Andes proclaims to us the beauty and happiness that comes from a pure heart."

POPE JOHN PAUL II, MARCH 21, 1993, CANONIZATION HOMILY

FEAST DAY: JULY 13

PATRONAGES: YOUTH, SICK PEOPLE

orn on July 13, 1900, in Santiago, Chile, to Miguel Fernandez Jarequemada and Lucia Solar Armstrong, little did newborn Juanita Fernandez Solar realize that she would one day become the first Carmelite saint from the Americas. Days later she was baptized Juana Enriqueta Josefina de los Sagrados Corazones on the feast of Our Lady of Mount Carmel. Named after her grandmothers, Saint Joseph, *and* the Sacred Hearts of Jesus and Mary, she was simply called Juanita by those who knew and loved her.

Juanita was close to her younger sister, Rebecca, and enjoyed spending time with her extended family. Hers was an affluent rural family who made a living through agriculture and spent part of their year on their large plantation. As she plainly explained in her diary regarding her family's finances, "Jesus did not desire me to be born poor like himself; I was born in the midst of riches, spoiled by all." As a child, brown-haired, blue-eyed Juanita was spoiled by her grandfather, who often took the grandchildren out to horseback ride. She also had a temper and would later describe incidents from her childhood as making her blood boil and bringing on a "ferocious fit of anger." Adding to the challenges of her upbringing, family members would openly say that Juanita was the prettiest of her siblings, much to her mother's disapproval. So as a child, Juanita could not be called perfect: she argued with her younger sister, Rebecca, and would dawdle when asked to do something. With such a tempera-

> **The feast of Our Lady of Mount Carmel** commemorates the occasion of the Virgin Mary's presentation to Saint Simon of the scapular (a garment worn by Carmelites and other monastics, which was originally in the shape of the cross).

Our Lady of Mount Carmel

ment and such surroundings, her parents knew Juanita was in danger of vanity, anger, and becoming ungrateful for her many gifts, so they strove to instill a strong faith in their daughter.

Age six saw Juanita going to daily Mass with her Aunt Juana. This regular, early exposure to the Mass inspired Juanita, who had also been influenced by the fear-inducing earthquake of 1906 to beg for first Communion from the Jesus who had taken "my heart to be his own." The adults in her life, however, felt that she was still too young. She also grew to have a devotion to the Virgin Mary. She and her brother, Luis, agreed to pray the rosary every day. Juanita later admitted that she only forgot her promise on one day. Years later, she gave a statue of Mary to her brother Luis, telling him in a letter, "So many times she comforted my heart when it was weighed down with sorrow."

Earthquake of 1906:
On August 16, 1906, a powerful earthquake rocked Valparaiso, Chile, leaving fires in its wake, thousands of people dead, and many more injured.

Finally, on September 11, 1910, at age ten, Juanita received her heart's desire of first Communion. The night before, she had participated in the sacrament of confession and afterward asked each person in her house, including servants, to forgive her for any wrongs that she had committed against them. After first Communion, she even gave some of the money she received as a gift to the poor.

For Juanita, Communion was a very special experience, and even more life-changing than it is for most young people. She would later share that Jesus began speaking to her after Communion and would continue to speak to her each time she received the Eucharist. "He told me things that I never dreamed of, and even when I asked him, he told me things that were to happen and they actually happened." Juanita did not realize for a long time how especially blessed she was to receive this gift. In fact, she thought everyone who received Christ in holy Communion had such vivid experiences.

Juanita enjoyed the typical schoolgirl life of someone of her background. While it was common for most young women at that time to attend boarding schools, Juanita spent many of her younger years living at home and attending school nearby. But from 1915–1918 Juanita was a high school boarding student along with about seventy-nine other teenage girls. It was not easy for her to get used to her new school, and Juanita said that the experience of acclimating to her new life was difficult. Like many teenagers, she dreaded going back to school after summer break, saying melodramatically, "The place is like a dungeon or a jail. The school should be reduced to ashes!"

How do you motivate yourself to get back into the swing of school after your summer break? What aspects of going to school do you miss over the summer?

Eventually her attitude toward high school changed. A generally good student, she had a challenging course load, studying English, handwriting, logic, metaphysics, psychology, the history of philosophy, religion, literature, chemistry, and ancient, medieval, modern, and Chilean history. Additionally, she could speak French and was skilled in Latin. Her favorite subjects were religion, literature, and philosophy, but she just couldn't seem to get herself to like chemistry. But for her parents' sake she was able to do her best and, in due course, achieved the best grade.

Juanita was involved in extracurriculars like the Children of Mary, an honorary religious group for young people. Juanita was a good friend. The tall girl was athletic, delighting in swimming, horseback riding, and tennis, but she also had a musical streak, even playing piano, guitar, and singing at family parties, as well as keeping a type of organ called a harmonium in her bedroom. She played this last instrument every morning, as she joyfully sang in prayer to God.

While Juanita was a girl who seemed to have everything that she needed, she was frequently sick and experienced the lingering negative effects of chloroform that had been given to her at age thirteen to ease the pain of appendicitis. She reflected that, "My life is composed of two things: suffering and love," but the suffering did not sadden her. On the contrary, she expressed her conviction that her suffering brought her closer to Jesus, who had suffered his whole life and in his death on the cross. In one of her mystical communications with Christ after receiving the Eucharist, he said to her, "...if you want to be like me, then take up your cross with love and joy." This would be her constant struggle.

With such mature and profound musings on suffering, it would be wrong to figure that suffering was always something easy for her to deal with. At age fourteen, on an occasion when she was ill, Juanita cried over being disregarded by the others in her household. In response, she heard a call from Christ to snap out of her funk. "I am alone on the altar of love of you, and can't you even suffer one moment of solitude? Juanita's appreciation of suffering also allowed her to better recognize and act to lessen the suffering of others. She especially sought to help the poor, who suffered from a lack of material things that she did not. She put her philosophies into practice by feeding, clothing, and finding shelter for an orphaned, begging little boy named Juanito; she took on his own suffering by giving him her dessert and selling her watch, as well as gifts she had received for her feast day, in order to buy him shoes.

Mystical: In the Catholic tradition, mysticism describes the desire of the soul for union with God. Teresa's "mystical communications with Christ grew out of her union with him, a union firmly rooted in the Eucharist.

The Fernandez family's great care for their children's needs masked their family hurdles. Juanita's parents did their utmost to provide for their household, like many parents do. Nonetheless, her father had unintentionally squandered the family money and was attempting to make it back. The result was that he was often away from home on business for extended periods of time. This, along with differences in her parents' personalities, caused tension between them. And Juanita deeply missed her dad, feeling left out that other girls got to spend time with their fathers. She would write letters pleading for him to come home to the family and asking him to go to Mass more regularly.

Feast day: In Juanita's and many other Catholic families, particularly those of Latin American origin, one's patron saint's feast day (many times a saint with the same name) was reason for real rejoicing; it was celebrated much like we mark our birthdays today.

In 1917, the teenage Juanita started her spiritual, mystical diary (*Diario Intimo*) at the behest of her spiritual director, Mother Julia Rios. She only shared that the diary existed to spiritual directors and select family members. Pretty soon after starting the diary, Juanita decided that she wanted to give herself to Christ as his spouse through the religious life. She wrote of her discernment that "only in God can I find happiness, the satisfaction of my desires, the possession of all good things, because he is truth and infinite goodness." After much discussion with her spiritual director, she took a permanent vow of chastity on December 8, the feast of the Immaculate Conception.

On her younger sister, Rebecca's, fourteenth birthday, Juanita wrote her a letter letting her know that she had finally made her decision. "You hear a voice and a light shows you the path of your life...That beacon shone for me when I was fourteen years old.

Diario Intimo: Available in an English translation (see Father Michael D. Griffin's *God, the Joy of My Life* on the source page), Juanita's *Diario Intimo* is a day-by-day accounting of her life as a Catholic teenager.

I changed my course and I determined the path that I had to follow."

Juanita felt that she had been lovingly called by Christ to a very great vocation: the salvation of others through prayer. She understood that as a religious sister, she would be a bride of Christ who "must be thirsty for souls," offering Christ, the bridegroom, "the blood that he shed for each soul."

At a time in life when many girls have a difficult time deciding who they even would like to go to the homecoming dance with, Juanita was taking steps toward becoming a religious sister through her vow of chastity. But even so, Juanita was a modern girl who got excited to get to see an airplane take off and took part in all the family parties, even though she was sometimes unsure of how to join in. While according to her older brother, Luis, he never saw her alone with any boys, she did have admirers.

Spiritual director: An individual who is trained, equipped, and sanctioned by the Church to lead a person or persons to a greater life of holiness. Think of spiritual directors as coaches for the people of God, leading us to strive for sainthood, which is eternal life with the Father.

One in particular brought her flowers and would walk with her around her neighborhood, although they never ended up courting or dating.

So instead of choosing which boy to date, one of Juanita's biggest adolescent struggles involved the decision of where she was called to enter the religious life. Should she join the women who had educated her in the Society of the Sacred Heart or go the ancient and mystical route of the Carmelites? At the time, she had never even met a Carmelite, however, she had learned about them through Saint Thérèse of Lisieux's *Story of a Soul*, Saint Teresa of Avila's *Autobiography*, and Blessed Elizabeth of the Trinity's *The Praise of Glory*. Carmelite spirituality called to her through the voices of these women. Juanita had an especial affinity for Saint Thérèse of Lisieux, and saw similarities in her own experience to Thérèse's. "Thérèse's soul has points in common with my own," Teresa would write. "Like her, I have received many favors from Our Lord that made her come to perfection in a short time; but I have repaid Jesus very poorly."

Thérèse's writings, as well as those of Elizabeth of the Trinity, inspired her to desire to be a "victim soul" by offering her suffering for others.

> **Vocation:** The word "vocation" comes from the Latin *vocare*, which means "to call." In short, a vocation is a call to the deepest desires of the human heart.

Juanita was plainly inspired by the spiritual guidance in all three of the holy women's writings, two of whom—Saint Teresa of Avila and Saint Thérèse of Lisieux—were each named Doctor of the Church during the twentieth century.

However, even with all her enthusiasm for the Carmelite way of life, Juanita was afraid she'd not be able to handle its rigors. Even her spiritual director, Mother Rios, questioned it, asking if her health was strong enough for her vocation. Juanita's response was to pray to Saint Thérèse that her health might be able to deal with it. Even though she was excited to have made her decision, she was worried and grieved about leaving her family, especially her mother and Rebecca, for the convent; her family's mixed reactions to her desire to become a Carmelite nun didn't make it any easier.

Saint Teresa of Avila

Saint Thérèse of Lisieux

It's OK to not be as sure regarding your vocational call as Juanita was when she was a teenager. What direction do you think you might be called to? How are you attempting to define your calling?

When she was seventeen, Juanita started writing back and forth with Mother Angelica of the Most Blessed Sacrament, the prioress of Los Andes. Because all twenty letters are still around, we know

that they shared everything—both the good and the bad. She would share little joys from her current life with her family, such as how much she enjoyed spending time with her newborn niece. We also know that Juanita revealed a deep understanding of the Carmelite life she was seeking to enter. She shared with the prioress that she was sure that it would be a life of suffering and of love, and told her that she had been taught these things by Jesus since a very young age.

Juanita at age eighteen.

August of 1918 found the eighteen-year-old moving from school back to the family home. By the end of her time in high school, times had certainly changed from her stark beginnings there—it turned out that she didn't want to leave! But Juanita was ready to go on to the next stage of her life and to more fully pursue her vocation.

The following January 11, Juanita and her mother took the train from Santiago to Los Andes to spend the day at the Carmelite monastery. The only other person who knew they were going was Rebecca—not even Juanita's father knew. The pair of women who had been accustomed to comfort came to a convent founded a little more than twenty years before their visit which was impoverished and simple, with neither electricity nor hot water. That seemed to only further endear Juanita.

Juanita later wrote joyfully of her experience of the visit. She recalled fondly her conversations with Mother Angelica, the woman to whom she had written so many letters. "Mother Angelica began to speak of the love of God with an eloquence that seemed to come from the depths of her soul," Juanita said. "She made me see the great goodness of God in calling me and how all that I was came from God." They spoke until 4:30 p.m., at which point they met the rest of the community, and each one of the Carmelite sisters greeted Juanita lovingly and affectionately—a huge surprise to the young woman! Juanita was met with approval and said she would come the first week of May—only four months away!

Three months later, on April 3, 1919, Juanita finally wrote to her father, who was living a distant three hundred miles to the south, asking for permission to enter the Carmel at Los Andes. She also requested that he give a tithe to her new community in the form of a dowry for the support of the poor convent. With her letter came a heartfelt belief that "those who love one another can never be separated!" Regardless, he was broken up over her request, knowing that, because the convent was cloistered, after her entrance into monastic life, he would likely never see her again. Sometime later, he finally gave Juanita her reply in person, telling her through tears that he could not oppose the will of God, especially since he knew it would make her happy. Juanita was ecstatic at his decision but had to tell her father that she would be leaving the very next month.

Even though it seemed that Juanita's path to Carmel was now clear, she found that her older brother, Luis, was very angry with both her decision and her parents' consent of it. He wrote her a letter trying to convince her against joining the monastery, saying he thought her abilities and looks would go to waste. His words did not sway Juanita's resolve, even as they made her departure more difficult. "I have no beauty," she humbly told her brother, "But if I

A dowry, or money provided by a woman's family in order to help provide for her household and family needs after she is married, was also generally expected of women entering religious life. This would have been especially important in Juanita's case, as she was entering a community of Carmelite women who lived extremely simply and would rely on the aid of her father's dowry to help provide for her.

did possess any, I wouldn't hesitate to offer that to him [Jesus], too, because the good and the beautiful is what he deserves." What followed was a spiritually difficult time in which she was so upset that she sought counsel from her confessor. "There is a dark cloud that is hiding the beloved of my heart and I long to plunge myself into his divine being, but I am unable to do so."

Sometimes a good decision isn't always met with friends' and family members' utter joy and validation. Share a time when you are sure you made the right call, but others didn't back you up at first. How did you react and stand firm with your resolution? Did those who opposed you come around?

Even with these struggles, Juanita continued her final preparations for her departure for the Carmel of Los Andes. Since cameras were not allowed in the monastery, she had her picture taken in a borrowed habit of a fully professed Carmelite sister (the type of which she would never actually end up living long enough to receive herself) and gave copies to her relatives and the convent, which would be her new family. Another issue on her mind was what to do with her diary. Her own preference was to destroy it before leaving her home, but she worried that in doing so she might deprive someone else of learning from her experiences. "If they do read it," she wrote, "they will see the goodness of the Divine Master who has loved me so much even though I have been so ungrateful and am so sinful, but even for that reason I would be glad if they did read it." The decision was finally made when a priest advised her to keep it.

When it came time to say goodbye,

Postulant: A man or woman's first step into religious life; the period of postulancy is characterized by a spirit of initial discernment and general introduction into the specific order and individual community's ways.

Novice: A person in the religious life interval known as novitiate (the next step after postulancy), a novice is one who is furthering his or her education and continuing discernment toward making a religious vow. By being allowed to finish the novitiate and take her vows early, Teresa died a professed Carmelite.

Juanita ate a parting dinner with her family and prepared to leave the next morning. Her dad couldn't bear to see her off, so on May 7, 1919, Juanita got up early, went to Mass, and took the train to the convent with her mom, her sister, Rebecca, her brother, Luis, Aunt Juana, as well as a friend, getting to Los Andes at 11:30 a.m. They had lunch in the little town and said their final goodbyes.

Five months into her stay at the Los Andes Carmel, Juanita took the name Sister Teresa of Jesus and received the postulant's habit of the Discalced Carmelites. It was October of 1919.

Less than a year later, during the early spring of 1920, Sister Teresa began to feel ill. Holy Week came, and on Holy Thursday, still feeling strangely sick, she spent extended hours in prayer. By Good Friday, she was highly feverish and ordered to bed by the novice mistress. She was so sick that her family was called and a doctor was sent for—she had contracted typhus. On Monday, April 5, she asked for the anointing of the sick, confession, and the Eucharist, and while the fever made her occasionally fall into incoherence, she was not in this state when, in the middle of the night, a little after midnight, she was offered the opportunity to take her vows as a Carmelite and thus die a professed Carmelite novice. Her last hours were filled with spiritual trials, such as periods of believing that God had cut her loose and disowned her.

On Monday, April 12, at 7:15 p.m., her physical and spiritual trials ended when, at the age of nineteen years and nine months, she died. Sister Teresa of Jesus had lived in the Carmelite monastery for eleven months.

PRAYER FOR THE INTERCESSION OF SAINT TERESA OF THE ANDES

God of mercy, joy of the saints,
you set the young heart of Blessed Teresa
ablaze with the fire of virginal love
for Christ and for his Church;
and even in suffering made her a cheerful witness to charity.
Through her intercession,
fill us with the delights of your Spirit
so that we may proclaim by word and deed
the joyful message of your love to the world.
We ask this through our Lord Jesus Christ, your Son,
who lives and reigns with you and the Holy Spirit,
one God, for ever and ever.
Amen.

MEMORY VERSE
I CORINTHIANS 13:13

So faith, hope, love remain, these three;
but the greatest of these is love.

How was the kind of love that Saint Teresa of the Andes lived both totally obedient and revolutionary at the same time? How does our greater society and world view this sort of love?

Saintly Challenges

- Teenage Juanita joined the Priestly Reparation Society, whose purpose was to pray for the needs of priests. Choose a priest, either from your own community or living somewhere else in the world, to lift up in prayer and perform a small sacrifice on his behalf and that of his ministry.

- Who is your patron saint and when is his or her feast day? Mark it on the calendar, brush up on his or her hagiography (a saint's biography), and plan some fitting way to celebrate!

- Movie night! Check out the Chilean-produced miniseries, shot in the style of a telenovela, called *Saint Teresa of the Andes*. Released by Ignatius Press with English subtitles, it gives a further look into her life as a teenager.

- Fry up some joy yourself, by making the tasty Chilean dish, cheese empañadas. (See the recipe on page 126.)

JOURNAL YOUR THOUGHTS

_____

_____

_____

_____

_____

_____

_____

_____

_____

_____

_____

_____

_____

_____

_____

_____

_____

_____

_____

_____

_____

_____

_____

_____

_____

_____

_____

_____

_____

SAINT KIZITO

HE BORE THE ULTIMATE WITNESS TO CHRIST

"Our hope and confidence—
like that of the holy martyrs who,
both in the south and the north of the country,
bore the ultimate witness to Christ—
are founded on the power of the risen Lord,
whose saving grace does not disappoint"
(Romans 5:5).

POPE JOHN PAUL II, MARCH 21, 1993, CANONIZATION HOMILY

FEAST DAY: JUNE 3

PATRONAGES: CHILDREN AND PRIMARY SCHOOLS

W e don't know much about the short life and childhood of Saint Kizito. Kizito, a member of the Muganda tribe, was born to Lukomera and Wangabira in the southern part of Uganda.

Important to Kizito's story is the prominence of Catholic missionaries in his home country. In 1879, when Kizito was still a very young child, the king of Buganda, Kabaka Mukabya, invited Catholic missionaries to his kingdom. A French priest, Cardinal Charles Lavigerie, sent the White Fathers on a fifteen-month journey to Uganda's Lake Victoria, where they were to serve as missionaries. From the time of their arrival, their mission strategy was to create larger missions in more densely populated areas, with smaller missions spread out across the countryside, about a day's journey from one another.

> **Buganda** is a kingdom located in the center of Uganda.

They had no idea that what awaited them would be an intense desire for the Faith in the missions of Uganda. Eventually, they decided that one must be catechized for two whole years before being allowed to be baptized. While this might sound unjust at first glance, it was really in the peoples' best interest, as they wanted to make sure that catechumens were converting for the right reasons and not just because they thought they might be better fed or met with greater prosperity by becoming Christian.

> **"Kabaka"** is the term for king In the kingdom of Buganda, Uganda.

Unfortunately, eventually the White Fathers would fall out of favor with Kabaka Mukabya. They were sent into exile from 1882 to 1885 and forced to abandon their catechumens until the king became more favorable to their missionary work among his people.

> **Catechumen:** A person learning about Christ and his Church who intends to be baptized into the Faith.

In 1885, Kabaka Mukabya died

> **White Fathers:** Originally called the White Fathers because of their white, traditionally Arab robes, they are now known as the Missionaries of Africa and continue to serve the needs of the people of the African continent.

and his son Mwanga became kabaka. Eager to increase the education in his kingdom, Kabaka Mwanga invited the missionaries to return, knowing that they would open schools for his people. He promised them safety and the liberty to teach the Faith at will. In addition, to prove that his regime was different from his father's, he put Christians, referred to as "the praying ones," into prominent places of power within the government of his kingdom. One notable young Christian man, Charles Lwanga, was appointed a royal page.

As a young teen, Kizito was also a page in the court of Kabaka Mwanga, and worked under the leadership of Charles Lwanga. But the new king began to share in his father's anger toward the Christians at that same time. He was not pleased with the morality of his Christian subjects. His head steward and leader of the palace's Christian community, Joseph Mukasa Balikuddembe, begged the kabaka to not force his male servants, including mere children, into impure acts. Kabaka Mwanga's response was to have Joseph killed on November 15, 1885. Mwanga's wrath spread to all other palace Christians who refused his advances, especially those who encouraged the more vulnerable teenage and young adult pages to be careful of his predilections.

After the martyrdom of Joseph Mukasa Balikuddembe, Mwanga then arrested and subsequently killed three Christians for no apparent reason other than their faith in Christ. At the same time, Mwanga tried to preserve his relationship with the White Fathers, trying to make amends for their deaths by upping his treatment of the Christian missionaries and even allowing them to meet with and teach the royal pages in the kabaka's audience chamber.

It was a dangerous time to be a Christian in the palace of the kingdom of Buganda.

Even with these dangers, many people still wanted to be baptized into the Christian faith. Around this time, the White Fathers changed their two-year waiting period for catechumans to four years. In the case of Charles Lwanga,

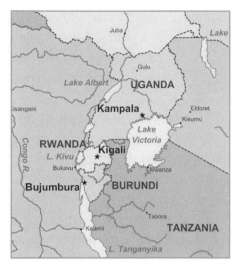

however, they made an exception and allowed him to be baptized right away on November 15, 1885; this was due to Charles' great zeal for Catholicism, as well as the danger he was now in as a Christian in a kingdom where martyrdom was a very real possibility. Even though Kizito begged, they refused to baptize him. He would have to wait.

By this time, it was evident to Uganda's Christian community that Mwanga was just as fickle and difficult to predict as his father. Mwanga equated the Catholic and Anglican missionaries with European attempts to take over his kingdom, and thus he was torn between his desire to educate his kingdom and his paranoia that they would attempt to unseat him from his throne. Additionally, he resisted Christianity's teachings against polygamy, pillaging, and massacring in war. Even in these difficult circumstances, the missionaries were enthusiastic about the success of the missions, observing that all of the kingdom seemed to be becoming Christian.

Despite the growing dangers, and while continuing to work in the kabaka's audience hall, fourteen-year-old Kizito was baptized along with

Polygamy: the practice of taking on more than one wife.

four other pages by Charles Lwanga, the head of the palace pages and new leader of its Christian community, in the early hours of May 26, 1886; it was especially courageous considering that Lwanga, only in his mid-twenties, had only been baptized himself the previous November.

Mwanga's anger toward the Christians would take an even deadlier turn. He had returned to his compound in a foul mood after a hippopotamus hunting trip and found all of his pages gone from the palace, with some of them in attendance at Christian prayer. He became even more irritated with fifteen of the pages' avoidance of his sexual advances, especially Kizito, Gyavira Musoke, and Mugagga Lubowa, the most honorable and handsome of the young men. In his rage, Mwanga decided to lock down the palace and summon them to answer whether they were Christians.

Mwanga had his pages, the chief executioner, and his assistant executioners brought to his presence so that the pages might answer to their Christian faith and unwillingness to act in sexual impurity with him. He demanded to know their chosen faith. When they all (including Kizito who had only just been baptized the previous night) bravely answered to their Christian faith, Mwanga had them tied up and proclaimed that they would all be burned, including the chief executioner's own nephew. The pages' spiritual leader, Father Lourdel, offered to Mwanga his life in return for the lives of Charles Lwanga, Kizito, and the rest of the pages, but Kabaka Mwanga refused.

Pillaging: to rob using violence, especially during wartime.

The pages were then bound together in their ropes and forced to walk thirty-seven miles north from Kampala to the site of their execution in the wooded area of Namugongo. Not content to kill the Christians quietly, the kabaka ordered they be led ceremonially over the roads, tied neck to neck, all the while continuing to pray and speak of the catechism lessons they had learned. Charles Lwanga led the group, and his peaceful attitude was shared by the other pages, even as they approached what they knew would be the place of their deaths. The fourteen-year-old, undersized Kizito, always known to have a happy disposition and entertain his fellow pages with music, was said to be laughing as he walked. Denis Kamyaka, a fellow page who made the journey to Namugongo to be executed but was later set free, remembered Kizito as incredibly joyful and not worried in the least about what the journey's end might hold.

When they were in the middle of their journey to the execution site, the pages came upon the chief executioner, a man named Senkole. He was there to strike the skull of each of those chosen to die (which was all of them except three) with a flame-tipped reed, in order, according to the paganism practiced by the king, to prevent the young men's souls from haunting the kabaka in the afterlife. This same Senkole, who oversaw the deaths of the Ugandan Martyrs, later became a catechumen himself.

A mural depicting the martyrdom of Saint Kizito.

Because Mwanga intended them to be examples of what would happen to those who crossed the king, he had representatives sent for from different areas of his kingdom to the place of execution, in order that they might go back to their homes and tell their neighbors

what they had seen. Their reports tell us that the martyrs were rolled up into straw mats and placed among the wood of the fire. Soldiers kept the fire moderated to prolong their suffering while being burned. In all, sixteen Catholics between the ages of thirteen and thirty-four were martyred that day, the feast of the Ascension.

The shrine of Saint Kizito.

PRAYER

*Mary, queen of peace! To you we commend the men,
women and children of Uganda.
Through your prayers, may the spirit of God
grant lasting peace and prosperity to their nation.
May the light of Christ cast out the spiritual darkness
which breeds selfishness, violence,
hatred for others and contempt for their rights.
May all hearts be opened to the power of God's love.
May those divided by ethnic or political antagonisms
learn to work together in order to build a society of justice,
peace, and freedom for their children. Amen.*

—An excerpt from John Paul II's 1993 Angelus address
at the Shrine of the Martyrs of Uganda in Namugongo, Kampala

MEMORY VERSE
ROMANS 5:5

*...Hope does not disappoint, because the love of
God has been poured out into our hearts through
the holy Spirit that has been given to us.*

*Write the name of a person living today who is working to build a society
of justice, peace, and freedom for their children: How does he/she do
this?*

Saintly Challenges

- If you were baptized as an infant or a young child, find out as much as you can about your own baptism from your parents and/or godparents, including how old you were, where it took place, who the celebrant was, and who else was there. In addition, track down your baptismal candle, certificate, and any garments you might have worn.

  If one doesn't already exist, create your own scrapbook of remembrances of each of your sacramental celebrations.

- Laugh! While this sounds easy enough, Kizito is the perfect witness of a saint who managed a smile on his face and laughter in his heart even in encountering literally mortal danger.

- See the film *Up!* This film poignantly treats serious life issues with a dose of humor. Be prepared to both tear up and guffaw until you snort.

- With the zeal of a new convert, fearlessly tell one person about your faith.

- Try matoke! (Recipe on page 127.) In Uganda, matoke is a staple food—it's one of those things visitors see enjoyed everywhere! If you were enjoying this with Kizito's family, it would be cooked over an open fire, but this recipe is more suited to the average American kitchen.

JOURNAL YOUR THOUGHTS

JOURNAL YOUR THOUGHTS

BLESSED CHIARA LUCE BADANO

A RAY OF LIGHT

Dear friends, only Love with a capital "L" can bring true happiness! This is shown by another witness....I am speaking of Chiara Badano.... Despite her suffering, she was a ray of light [luce] as her nickname suggests, "Chiara Luce."

POPE BENEDICT XVI, ANGELUS, SEPTEMBER 26, 2010

FEAST DAY: OCTOBER 29

After eleven years of praying for a child, Ruggero and Maria Theresa Badano were blessed with the life of newborn Chiara on October 29, 1971, in Sassello, a mountain town outside Savona, Italy. Ruggero, a quiet truck driver with tenacious faith, was from a family with a cloth business, while the very outgoing Maria Theresa grew up with seven brothers and sisters in a family that struggled just to get by, especially so after their house caught on fire and burned to the ground. But throughout the years that they yearned for a child, Maria Theresa and Ruggero clung to their faith and trusted in God's plan. Later, Maria Theresa would reflect that she considered all of their struggles "to be the will of God. He loved me, and so this inability to have children was love, too."

Chiara's mother decided to be a stay-at-home mom because she believed it was her role to teach her daughter to love. So Chiara's childhood has been remembered as one spent playing, appreciating nature, and serving those of God's people who are forgotten or neglected by most others, all with her mother close by. Having gone to Mass with her parents since she was a baby, by kindergarten, she was saving money for African missions and dreaming of one day being a medical doctor there. In elementary school, Chiara would give her snack away to a less fortunate classmate, and when her mother realized what she was doing and started packing two snacks, she gave twice as much away.

Her parents, seri-

cBLESSED CHIARA LUCE cBADANO

ously considering their daughter's status as an only child, made a concerted effort not to spoil her and to raise her well. Chiara would occasionally clash with her mom or dad over things like doing various chores, giving some toys away to charity, or saying her prayers, as many kids do. But it never took her long to come around and choose on her own, without too much parental pressure, to obey them. Both of her parents were motivated by love in parenting the young girl. While her mother knew that it was her duty to educate Chiara, she knew that "first of all I had to pass love on to her." Her father was of the same mind, and while he might have been viewed as strict, he said, "I always did it out of love, always; never out of spite or tiredness or any other reason."

Nevertheless, she wasn't a perfect kid—she once took an apple from a neighbor's property without permission, and her mother made her take it back and apologize. Her parents' vigilance in keeping their daughter honest and Chiara's atonement for her actions were later rewarded when her neighbor brought over a whole basket of apples for her to have.

At age nine, she became involved in Focolare's youth movement, Gen (New Generation). Focolare would play a pivotal role in the rest of her short life, and Chiara was deeply influenced by the Catholic ecumenical movement's founder, Chiara Lubich, quoting her often

Focolare: Started in Italy during World War II, Focolare, whose name is derived from the Italian word for a home's fireplace, is an international movement recognized by the Church that bases its mission on the Gospel. In particular, the movement draws from Jesus' prayer in the Gospel of John 17:20–21: "I pray not only for them, but also for those who will believe in me through their word, so that they may all be one, as you, Father, are in me and I in you, that they also may be in us, that the world may believe that you sent me." Members of Focolare work toward Jesus' prayer that all people may be one.

and writing her letters. The spirituality of Focolare emphasizes the image of the forsaken Christ as something to be embraced and loved as a means of making it through the rougher patches of life, and the young Chiara would take this to heart. By the time she was twelve, not even old enough to date or drive, Chiara was already proclaiming in writing that, "...I have made a new resolution to see Jesus forsaken as my spouse and to welcome him joyfully and, above all, with all the love possible." From this early acceptance of his cross, she was able to stay strong later, when she would be tested to the limit both physically and spiritually.

Teased because she went to Mass, attended religious education classes, and made herself available to help anyone, such as sick friends and their relatives, kids would pick on Chiara, calling her "Sister." But even with all her religious devotion and commitment to service, it would be wrong to assume that she didn't make time for entertainment and friends. For this extroverted girl, "fun" involved spending time listening to pop music, singing, dancing, as well as tennis, hiking in the mountains, and swimming at the beach. According to her pal, Lucia, Chiara was always full of life, and her friends could see her purity and vitality through her smile and in her eyes. Chiara tried to be very sensible and level-headed about her relationships with boys, trying to make sure that she was involved in the right way and for the right reasons.

Ecumenical: A Christian movement emphasizing the unity of all people of faith.

That same year, her family moved from their village of Sassello to the bigger town of Savona to be closer to Ruggero's job and Chiara's school, coming back to Sassello for the weekends. Even though she worked hard, she wasn't naturally the most gifted student, even failing some of her classes. A teacher once commented to Chiara's mother that she thought Chiara would be a judge or a lawyer, owing to her ardent defense of the pope when the teacher herself criticized him for the costs of his many trips. In her struggles at school and concerns about her future, as well as in her negotiations with her parents on her curfew, she dealt with problems and stresses common to many teenagers today.

What area of your life where, even though you work hard, you still struggle to excel?

In November 1985, when she was fourteen and in the fall of her first year of high school, Chiara decided that the extraordinary message of the Gospels would become the focus of her life. She went to daily Mass as much as possible and followed the countercultural path of a Catholic teenager, seeking to live a life of action and witness. Dedicating her actions to him, Chiara once said, "It is so hard to go against the current! For you, Jesus!" However, in the face of that difficulty, Chiara Badano believed that "young people have only one life to live, and it is worthwhile to spend it well."

Vitality: Energetic; full of life.

Like her namesake, Saint Clare of Assisi, she was a girl of action. She wasn't content to go through the motions or to just say that she was a Christian. She felt compelled to dedicate her life to Christ. "I should not speak about God, but give to him with my behavior," Chiara said of the Gospel life we are all called to. When others failed to act to see Christ in their neighbors, Chiara would stand ready to remind them. There was a boy with a cognitive disability at Chiara's parish who would sing loudly, disturbing other Mass-goers in the church. One day, he asked Chiara's mother to sit with him. When she later told Chiara what had happened, Chiara told her that she knew that Jesus was present in that boy. At Chiara's death, that same boy took off his hat, kissed her feet, and recited the entirety of the rosary without any assistance.

In the summer of 1988, Chiara experienced searing pain in her arm and shoulder while playing tennis. Realizing that something was not right, she and her family consulted a doctor to determine what was wrong. Though they initially thought she had cracked her rib, her diagnosis would be much more serious. At age seventeen, osteosarcoma with metastasis, a type of bone cancer, had been found. In the face of excruciating, constant pain, Chiara's attitude was nothing if not brave. "It's for you, Jesus; if you want it, I want it, too," Chiara would say, referring to her pain.

She was so intent on being fully aware of her surroundings and her own suffering that she refused the morphine the doctors offered, explaining that it would have the negative effect of keeping her from lucidity. It was important to Chiara that she be aware of her illness and the pain it caused, so that she could offer her suffering to Jesus.

Her ability, through her love of God, to handle the seemingly bleak prospects that the bone cancer brought with it enabled her to bring the message of Christ's peace to other patients, as well as the doctors looking after her in the hospital. The doctors used adjectives like "unnatural" and "incredible" to describe Chiara's attitude and witness in the face of her illness. One of the medical professionals who grew to know her, Dr. Antonio Delogu, later said, "She showed with her smile, with her big luminous eyes, that death doesn't exist—only life exists."

Lucidity: the state of being in possession of one's faculties or mind.

Ruggero, her father, shared that Chiara reached out by helping another young patient who was suffering from depression. Chiara would often go on long walks with the young girl to comfort her, even when she should have been resting for her own health. When her parents told her that she needed to get her rest, Chiara would reply, "I'll be able to sleep later on."

During her sickness, Chiara Badano would write letters back and forth with her spiritual mentor, Chiara Lubich. A practice common to Focolare is the taking of a new name as a symbol of a new faith journey in Christ. As a result, Chiara Badano wrote Chiara Lubich for a suggestion for her own new name. Lubich wrote her the first of many letters, telling the young Chiara that "your luminous face shows your love for Jesus" and giving her the nickname "Luce," meaning "light." In a letter in 1989, Lubich also encouraged her with the message that she would bear much fruit in her life, an allusion to Jesus' message in John 15:5–8:

> *I am the vine, you are the branches. Whoever remains in me and I in him will bear much fruit, because without me you can do nothing. Anyone who does not remain in me will be thrown out like a branch and wither; people will gather them and throw them into a fire and they will be burned. If you remain in me and my words remain in you, ask for whatever you want and it will be done for you. By this is my Father glorified, that you bear much fruit and become my disciples.*

How are you bearing fruit in your own life?

Throughout her illness, Chiara dealt with the crosses being laid upon her shoulders with grace, growing closer to Jesus through them. It could have been a time of alienation and bitterness, but instead she used it to deepen her union with him. She constantly tried to keep the focus off of herself by thinking of others, even in the midst of her suffering. She donated all of her birthday money to a friend heading to the West African country of Benin to dig wells for clean water and went out of her way to do kind things for her family.

When Valentine's Day rolled around, Chiara wanted her parents to go out. Since she was quite ill by this point, they resisted leaving her, and since they hadn't made dinner reservations, she did so from her bed and told them not to come home before midnight. Chiara was preparing her parents for the approaching time when she would have to leave them, urging them to not let their marital relationship suffer in the preoccupation and worry revolving around her illness. She even wrote them a Christmas card, hidden away in a pile of blank ones she knew her mother would eventually use, saying, "Holy Christmas 1990. Thank you for everything. Happy New Year," to find as a comfort to them after she had gone to meet Jesus.

There came a point in her illness when Chiara realized that she would probably never get better. Chiara trusted that when she died, her suffering would end and she would go to heaven. She began planning what she hoped would be a joyful celebration—her funeral—with this in mind. She spoke of being buried in her wedding dress (white with a pink waistband), because death was her chance to become the bride of Christ. In the last hours of her short life, she received the sacraments of confession and the Eucharist, and asked for those around her bedside to pray "Come Holy Spirit" with her. Her last words, "Bye, Mom. Be happy, because I am," were her way of comforting her mother and letting her know how much she was looking forward to meeting Jesus and spending eternity with him in heaven.

Chiara Lubich: (1920-2008) Born Sylvia Lubich, this woman behind the international Focolare Movement experienced a conversion of the heart in her early twenties that led her to adopt the name Chiara (Italian for Clare and a reference to Saint Clare of Assisi) and spend the rest of her life working toward the unity of the human family.

Chiara Luce Badano died at 4 in the morning on October 7, 1990, the feast of Our Lady of the Rosary. She was laid out in her wedding dress in her parents' house, where people visited and prayed the rosary. On the day of her October 9 funeral, the mayor of Sassello shut down all the shops of the town so that more than two thousand people could attend the service. They were singing, and as Chiara Luce had said, "I will be singing with you."

At Chiara Badano's September 26, 2010, beatification ceremony, a large picture of her was unveiled. What makes it unique is that it could be a senior picture from any contemporary American high school's yearbook. With her hair pulled back into a ponytail and yet at the same time wildly askance, framing a joyful smile and bright, lively eyes, she could easily be anyone's best friend, classmate, or girlfriend.

PRAYER: COME, HOLY SPIRIT!

The prayer that Chiara Luce prayed with her family
and friends in her last earthly moments with them.

Come, Holy Spirit, come!
And from your celestial home
Shed a ray of light divine!
Come, Father of the poor!
Come, source of all our store!
Come, within our bosoms shine.
You, of comforters the best;
You, the soul's most welcome guest;
Sweet refreshment here below;
In our labor, rest most sweet;
Grateful coolness in the heat;
Solace in the midst of woe.
O most blessed Light divine,

Shine within these hearts of yours,
And our inmost being fill!
Where you are not, we have naught,
Nothing good in deed or thought,
Nothing free from taint of ill.
Heal our wounds, our strength renew;
On our dryness pour your dew;
Wash the stains of guilt away:
Bend the stubborn heart and will;
Melt the frozen, warm the chill;
Guide the steps that go astray.
On the faithful, who adore
And confess you, evermore
In your sevenfold gift descend:
Give them virtue's sure reward;
Give them your salvation, Lord;
Give them joys that never end.
Amen. Alleluia!

MEMORY VERSE
JOHN 15:8

"By this is my Father glorified, that you bear much fruit and become my disciples."

Do you spend time with other people who are "bearing fruit" and thus glorifying God? If so, how are they? If your friends aren't, how is this affecting your own faith life?

Saintly Challenges

- From a young age, Chiara Luce had a heart for the African missions, especially those in the West African country of Benin, whose people were represented at her beatification Mass.

  On her October 29 feast day (or any other day), commemorate Chiara's life's passion for action in the name of Christ by donating the money you would spend on one week's worth of soda (or school lunch dessert or something else that's non-essential that you could fast from) to Catholic Relief Service's projects in Benin.

- Chiara died on October 7, the feast of Our Lady of the Rosary, which commemorates the Christian victory at the Battle of Lepanto. Observe the day by praying a rosary for teens who, like Chiara did, are battling bone cancer.

  Monday and Saturday—The Joyful Mysteries
  Tuesday and Friday—The Sorrowful Mysteries
  Wednesday and Sunday—The Glorious Mysteries
  Thursday—The Luminous Mysteries

- The Badano family's relationship was very close, having a devotion to each other with love of God at its center. Demonstrate the great care you have for your own family by giving whoever usually makes dinner the night off from cooking and making this dish of green tastiness to share with them. (See page 128 for the recipe.)

JOURNAL YOUR THOUGHTS

JOURNAL YOUR THOUGHTS

SAINT STANISLAUS KOSTKA

AN EXAMPLE OF FORTITUDE

"I wish to point out to you, too, the example of fortitude of a young eighteen-year-old, Saint Stanislaus Kostka, the patron saint of students, who, to follow his vocation to the religious state, though of a frail constitution and sensitive nature, faced the opposition of his circle, fled from the pursuit of his relatives, and traveled on foot, secretly, from Vienna to Rome, in order to enter the novitiate of the Jesuits and thus answer the Lord's call."

POPE JOHN PAUL II, NOVEMBER 15, 1978,
ADDRESS TO YOUNG PEOPLE IN SAINT PETER'S BASILICA

FEAST DAY: NOVEMBER 13

PATRONAGES: STUDENTS, POLAND, LIFE-THREATENING ILLNESSES tanislaus Kostka was born the second of seven children in September 1550, on the Kostka family estate in Masovia, Poland. The son of a Catholic noble family, his father was a Polish senator and his mother was related to various Polish officials, including the country's chancellor. Baptized in Saint Adalbert Church in Prasnitz, his godfather carried him to the tabernacle and dedicated the baby to Christ. Of average height, with black hair, a full face, rugged physique and pale skin, Stanislaus was a child who looked old for his age.

His parents raised their children in the Catholic faith from a young age, ensuring that they were taught the teachings of the Church and seeking to instill in them the virtues. It was challenging to raise children to be generous and not self-indulgent, especially with such a wealthy upbringing.

But Stanislaus' older brother, Paul, would later report that his parents' strict approach succeeded with their children, teaching them to become pious and virtuous young people so that not even the servants complained about their behavior. "The result was that we showed respect to everyone, as to our parents, and were loved by all." It was this practice of faith and virtue that Stanislaus learned from such a young age that followed him throughout the rest of his life.

How did your family handle discipline when you were a kid? Would you go the same route with your own children? Why or why not?

As a child, Stanislaus began practicing the virtues his parents had taught him. Whenever guests' dinner conversation would go in a lewd direction, Stanislaus would look down and not participate. Eventually, he mastered how to move the exchanges with peers from the disturbing or profane to subjects more appropriate for Christians. But at a younger age, he would be deeply affected. Often Stanislaus would gaze up and, seemingly unaware of his surroundings, fall to the ground. This happened frequently throughout his life, and, fortunately, his father was understanding of this and thus tried to keep the talk to less vulgar subjects.

How do you usually handle situations where people are discussing things they shouldn't? Does your reaction square with the way you know you should respond? How so?

Paul and Stanislaus were home-schooled by their teacher, John Bilinski, until 1564, when the teenagers, John, and three servants went to Vienna to study in a new college run by the Society of Jesus with other students from across Europe. The other students soon recognized the holiness of fourteen-year-old Stanislaus, as he enjoyed quietness, attending vespers prayers, venerating Mary, and, if possible, attending three Masses a day; no doubt due in large part to his example, two of these classmates became a cardinal and an archbishop. Several witnesses also even attested on various occasions to have seen Stanislaus levitate while serving Mass or in the midst of the joy of prayer.

> **Levitate:** The means by which a being or thing, in this case a saint, is lifted into the air through the miraculous power of God.

> **Society of Jesus:** Founded by Saint Ignatius Loyola in the sixteenth century, the Society of Jesus was responsible for founding many educational institutions across Europe during Stanislaus' time for the purpose of teaching Catholic doctrine. Their motto, *"Ad majorem Dei gloriam,"* or "to the greater glory of God," captures the society's spirit of working for God's glory in efforts big and small. Today the Jesuits are the largest single religious order of priests and brothers in the world.

What kind of example of Christian living are you to your friends and schoolmates?

In March 1565, not long after their arrival at the Jesuit school, the building was closed and students were forced to move out or to find another place to live. Paul Kostka and John Bilinski decided that they would all move into a house, sharing a room with two other noble young Polish men. This decision would have an impact on Stanislaus' teenage life.

John Bilinski's main job as tutor for the sons of one of the top families of Poland was to educate Stanislaus and his brother, Paul, on all the manners and expectations of a proper nobleman. But Stanislaus didn't enjoy the things that noble young men were supposed to practice, such as dressing extravagantly and dancing, and he tried to avoid having a servant with him. Unfortunately, John didn't help matters, for he felt that Stanislaus' life wasn't proper to a nobleman and he should be more attuned to society's expectations for someone from his background. Paul more than made up for him in those respects,

Jesuit: a common term referring to a member of the Society of Jesus or an organization established by the society.

as he was a partier who enjoyed the perks of a noble's life and didn't regularly go to Mass or live his life as a faithful Catholic. In Stanislaus, Paul saw everything that he wasn't, and he hated him for it.

Frequently, when Stanislaus stayed up praying, his roommates would get annoyed that the candle was burning so late. They'd pretend not to see him and kick and fall over him, but Stanislaus didn't react. The injustices seemed to make Stanislaus' spiritual life stronger. Once, he fell asleep and his candle burned down to the end, setting fire all around him in his bed. When his roommates awoke, they were sure he must be burned, but, shockingly, he was perfectly fine.

Due to his piety, Stanislaus' brother and tutor despised him, calling him "the Jesuit" as an insult, and from the time they moved out of the Jesuit dormitories into the private residence, Paul became violent. For almost two and a half years, he assaulted his brother, striking him with a stick, kicking, and often trampling him, and while John Bilinski sometimes intervened, he always seemed to blame Stanislaus for his own abuse, never reproving Paul himself.

How do you usually handle people wronging you? What could you learn from Stanislaus' approach? Do you think it would be helpful in your situation? Why or why not?

In response to the afflictions brought on by Paul and others, Stanislaus consistently turned the other cheek and put up with all that they subjected him to. He would always try to do what Paul asked of him, as well as performing chores such as sweeping, and cleaning Paul's shoes. He also made the concession that he would take a servant anywhere but to the church or to visit the Jesuits. However, this wasn't enough for Paul and John. In view of the fact that they thought he might run away and join the Society of Jesus, they had servants follow Stanislaus wherever he went. If the servants were able to find him, he was typically in the church, lying on the ground and extending out his arms into a cross. Sometimes, he was even found levitating. When the servants found him, Stanislaus would tell them not to be frightened as he tried not to draw attention to himself.

By the age of sixteen, the serious, calm young man had developed a spiritual routine that sustained him through his struggles. He went to Mass daily, usually three times a day (before and after his first class, as well as after school). He went to confession on Sundays and special feast days. In addition, he visited Christ in the Eucharist, often praying in adoration throughout the night before the tabernacle.

Stanislaus' difficult life at the Jesuit college began to take its toll.

By December 1566, Stanislaus had become ill, as a result of both his rigorous spiritual discipline as well as the abuse perpetrated by his brother. During this period, he suffered not only physically but spiritually. Stanislaus found himself visited three times by the devil in the form of a huge, black dog. But there was little he could do to fend off these spiritual attacks. Because he was living in the house of a Lutheran man who was virulently anti-Catholic, Communion or even a priest were not allowed into the house. God provided for the young saint, however; as later told by Stanislaus, Saint Barbara and two angels brought him Communion.

He also received in this vision an insight into his own vocation: Mary brought the child Jesus to his bed and laid him down, a sign he took to mean that he should seek to enter the Society of Jesus.

When Stanislaus recovered, he went to the church to offer thanks. His next step was to ask to enter the Jesuit order. While the teenager had felt the call to join the Society of Jesus for a while already, he hadn't because he was shy and didn't believe his father would allow him to. His illness changed all that. He went to a Jesuit at his school to tell him of his calling and that he was ashamed for not coming forward sooner and then requested the society's provincial in Vienna, Father Lorenzo Maggi, to accept him into the order. To Stanislaus' sorrow, he was denied without his powerful father's consent, seeing that they were worried about the repercussions of going against his will. It was then that

Saint Peter Canisius: (1521-1597) A Doctor of the Church born not long after Martin Luther's writing of the *95 Theses*, Dutch Saint Peter Canisius joined the Society of Jesus while in his twenties and is well-known for his work to help reevangelize and catechize a Germany split by the Reformation.

Stanislaus decided to travel to various Jesuit colleges, asking at each for permission to enter the order, and not returning to Poland until he had succeeded in his goal.

In August 1567, the seventeen-year-old Stanislaus met with Jesuit Father Francis Antoni regarding his predicament. Father Antoni understood that Stanislaus wasn't trying to be rebellious and encouraged him to petition Father Peter Canisius in Augsburg, Germany, and, if that didn't work, he should go to Rome and talk to the Jesuit general in charge of the entire order, Father Francis Borgia.

Meanwhile, Stanislaus' challenges with his brother continued, even as the young man knew he wouldn't have to bear it much longer. The next time Paul got on his case, Stanislaus did something out of character, telling him his maltreatment would cause him to leave. Paul didn't care, and told Stanislaus he didn't want to see any more of his brother. This was just the kind of "blessing" Stanislaus had anticipated; early the next morning, he had a simple set of traveling clothing ready to go, went to Mass in the Jesuit church, picked up his letters of reference and a blessing from Father Antoni, and had a servant tell his brother and tutor that he wouldn't be able to eat dinner with them, as he'd been invited somewhere else. He hit the open road.

Later that evening, Paul and John went looking for Stanislaus at the Jesuits' place, thinking he'd fled there. The Jesuits figured he'd headed to Rome, so Paul and John went off in a carriage to find him, stopping after ten miles without success. Stanislaus later reported that they had indeed caught up with him along the way but had not recognized him. Paul and John turned back for Vienna, thinking Stanislaus had gone by a different route. The next morning, they started out again, only to realize that they had passed him earlier and needed to turn around to go back and find him. But miraculously, the horses refused to move forward until they went in the opposite direction of the teenager. At that point, Paul and John decided they wouldn't try to fight against God's will. Paul Kostka began to regret his previous actions toward his brother.

When Paul wrote to his father, John Kostka, to tell him everything that had happened with Stanislaus' escape, his father became irate at both Stanislaus and the Society of Jesus and wrote threatening letters to both his runaway and a Polish bishop. When he got the letter from his father, Stanislaus read that he had shamed the family by dressing as a commoner and that John would come to Rome and get him to go back to Poland, where he would be held in imprisonment. Stanislaus did not write back in anger, but innocently asked why his joining the Jesuits made him so angry. Even so, he let his father know that he would not willingly be leaving the society.

Saint Francis Borgia: (1510-1572) Born into a noble family, Francis was a duke, a husband, and father of eight children by the time he was in his mid-thirties. However, his wife died, and he made the decision to enter the Society of Jesus. He not only became a Jesuit but was later named its superior general.

While journeying the four hundred fifty miles from Vienna to Augsburg, the nobleman Stanislaus Kostka prayed the rosary as he walked up to thirty miles a day, stopping at roadside chapels, and, as he did not have money, being forced to beg for his food. When he got to Augsburg and went looking for the Jesuit Provincial Father Peter Canisius at the Jesuit College, to his dismay he found out he was in Dillingen, Germany. Instead of stopping to rest, Stanislaus continued on, walking an entire day, along with a Jesuit companion, in order to get to him. When he arrived, Father Canisius was ready to accept him into the order, but Stanislaus was worried about the close proximity to Poland, so Father Peter made plans for him to

Originally built in the fourth century, the Basilica of Saint Maria Maggiore is one of the four major basilicas of Rome (The others are Saint Peter, Saint John Lateran, and Saint Paul Outside-the-Walls). According to tradition, Mary appeared and indicated that a church should be built on the spot through the sign of a snowfall in August. Referred to as the Miracle of the Snows, it is remembered every August 5 by a shower of white rose petals at the end of Mass.

eventually travel to Rome with two other Jesuits. Stanislaus would be a Jesuit—it would just take time.

In the meantime, Father Peter had Stanislaus, the young man of noble birth, take on menial tasks common to a Jesuit novice, such as serving the students of the school. On September 18, 1567, Father Peter wrote to Saint Francis Borgia, the head of the Jesuit order, that Stanislaus would soon be on his way to Rome. He described the young man as "a very good young Polish noble who is anxious to embrace our rule of life, even though his relations are against his doing so."

A Jesuit novice in Rome for about ten months, Stanislaus' day was highly structured (see page 69).

Stanislaus spent the last months of his life keeping the rules and Jesuit life perfectly and obediently. When talk of his nobility came up, he always changed the direction of the conversation, and he humbly worked to think before speaking. His was a totally absorbing prayer life, and he would frequently pass out and shake in the midst of his devotions, to the extent that he would have to apply a wet washcloth to his chest to relieve the literal feverishness from his great love of God.

The Jesuits were concerned about Stanislaus' weak health, and in the summer, he began passing out more regularly. By August, Stanislaus predicted among his fellow novices that he would die by the end of the month. At the time, his health seemed fine, but on August 5, when he went to the church of Saint Maria Maggiore, Stanislaus

Stanislaus' Daily Schedule as a Jesuit Novice

- awakened by bell
- half-hour of prayer
- dress
- make bed
- hour of prayer
- half-hour analyzing successes and failures of prayer
- Mass
- half-hour class or work from previous day's class
- half-hour discussion of lecture or work from previous day's class
- examination of conscience
- chores
- memorization work: Society of Jesus rules, catechism
- physical exercise
- lunch
- one hour of recreation
- homework/self-study period
- two hours of group study, memorizing catechism or working on homiletics
- half-hour of exercise
- half-hour of prayer
- dinner
- one hour of recreation
- examination of conscience
- bed

shared with his companion that he believed he would be in heaven to celebrate the feast of the Assumption of Mary on August 15. He petitioned the Blessed Mother to allow him to be with her in heaven on the feast of the Assumption and asked Saint Lawrence, his chosen patron for the month of August, to also petition Mary on his behalf. Later, as Stanislaus washed dishes, he began to feel sick and went to lie down. He was not violently ill for the following two days, but had a small fever. On Sunday, August 14, he told a Jesuit brother he would die the next evening, and, sure enough, by the middle of the day he started to become very sick and passed out.

It was then that those around him realized he was gravely ill. When he had confessed and received Communion, he received the anointing of the sick, made another confession, and held the crucifix. He had previously begged to be put on the ground, in order to die in total humility, but was refused until his last hours, when his request was granted. It was there that he laid and prayed continuously into the early hours of the feast of the Assumption, when he told those around him he was having a vision of Mary coming and meeting him in order to usher him to heaven. He died with a smile on his face between 3 and 4 in the morning.

But the story doesn't end there, as perhaps one of the greatest miracles of Saint Stanislaus' witness was the tremendous effect his life had on his older brother. Paul Kostka had journeyed to Rome to bring his brother back to Poland, not knowing that Stanislaus had already died the month before. Having wept at his tomb, he went back home and gave his family the news. Thereafter, his life changed. He lived and dressed simply, performed penances, prayed, and lived devoutly. He would lie on the floor of the church in the sign of the cross, as Stanislaus once had, and would cry any time he heard his brother's name. Later in life, he gave one of his estates to the Polish Jesuits and also created a hospital, working to serve the needy there. At age fifty-eight, Paul Kostka, the brother and tormentor of the first beatified Jesuit, asked to join the Society of Jesus. He was accepted, however, while wrapping up his affairs, he became sick and died.

Saint Stanislaus was beatified in 1605, while his brother was still alive, and later canonized on December 31, 1726.

PRAYER: PSALM 57:8-12

This is the psalm that Saint Stanislaus
proclaimed while in his final hours on earth.

My heart is steadfast, God, my heart is steadfast.
I will sing and chant praise.
Awake, my soul; awake, lyre and harp! I will wake the dawn.
I will praise you among the peoples,
LORD; I will chant your praise among the nations.
For your love towers to the heavens;
your faithfulness, to the skies.
Show yourself over the heavens, God;
may your glory appear above all the earth.
Amen.

MEMORY VERSE
PSALM 57:8

"My heart is steadfast, God, my heart is steadfast.
I will sing and chant praise."

Is your own heart devoted and ready to meet the Lord? Do you sing or chant praise? How do you go about honoring and calling upon God?

Saintly Challenges

- While a Jesuit novice in Rome, Stanislaus had a routine formulated to keep himself in good spiritual, physical, intellectual, and emotional shape. Take the time to plan out a good, basic, daily schedule for yourself that takes into account these same things. Take a day and try to keep to it. Then make any adjustments you might need to, and try to keep it for a whole week. Journal how it goes.

  Did you feel you were using your time more wisely? What kinds of struggles did you face in keeping to it? Do you have the discipline to keep it up for another week?

- Saint Stanislaus' humility in the face of the afflictions dealt out by his brother is truly remarkable. The next time you have a family squabble, emulate Saint Stanislaus, and, in the wake of it, do a simple, charitable act for the person, such as washing the dishes or making his bed. Better yet, do it on the sly!

- One way Saint Stanislaus used his time wisely was with nightly spiritual reading. He especially enjoyed books on Mary. Pick up your own devotional book on Mary.

- Saint Stanislaus and his teacher, John Bilinski, didn't always get along. This week, pray for an authority figure that you don't have the best relationship with. Ask God to do his best to help you improve your mutual understanding.

JOURNAL YOUR THOUGHTS

JOURNAL YOUR THOUGHTS

SAINT ALPHONSA OF THE IMMACULATE CONCEPTION

SHE CONFORMED HER LIFE TO CHRIST'S

She "...was convinced that her cross
was the very means of reaching
the heavenly banquet prepared
for her by the Father."

POPE BENEDICT XVI, HOMILY UPON THE CANONIZATION
OF SAINT ALPHONSA, SUNDAY, OCTOBER 12, 2008

FEAST DAY: JULY 28

PATRONAGE: SICK PEOPLE

aint Alphonsa was born on August 19, 1910, outside the town of Kottayam, India, the fourth child of Joseph Muttathupadathu and Mary Puthukari. Alphonsa's entrance into the world was an exciting one for a girl who would lead such a quiet life. When her mom, Mary, was still eight months pregnant with her, it was tremendously hot outside, so she decided to sleep on a mat in the courtyard of her house, along with her sister, Annamma. When she awoke, she found that a tropical snake had wrapped itself around her neck! She grabbed the snake and threw it off of herself, but, due to the fright, she went into immediate labor and delivered her daughter prematurely. A few weeks later, Mary tragically died.

Alphonsa's Syrian Christian parents could trace their family's faith all the way back to the Apostle Thomas' preaching in Malabar, India. They were members of the Syro-Malabar Catholic Church, which is in full communion with the Catholic Church but celebrates the liturgy according to its own language and form. In keeping with her family's strong tradition of Christian faith, she was baptized under the name Anna Muttathupadathu a little over a week after she was born, in the village of Kudamalur, India's Saint Mary's Church, but she was called "Annakutty," which is a nickname, like "Annie."

After her mother's death, Annakutty's family lived in her grandparents' home. There, her grandmother taught her about Mary and the saints, especially Saint Teresa of Avila and Saint Thérèse of Lisieux, and her father set an example of faith. By the age of five, she was actually leading the family's evening prayers! On November 27, 1917, upon receiving first Communion, she declared, "Do you know why I am so happy today? It is because I have Jesus in my heart!"

As a girl, Annakutty faced challenges and experiences we can relate to today. As a child, she faced the challenge of a serious illness. Her bouts with physical illness started early. Between the ages of three and four she had such extreme eczema, a skin disease, that it was thought that it would be terminal. But this experience would

SAINT ALPHONSA OF THE IMMACULATE CONCEPTION

not hold her back from living life to the fullest. She went to public school, where she befriended a Hindu girl named Lakshmikutty. Although they came from different backgrounds, the two best friends were notably known to ignore the rules against people of differing social classes eating together, in order to enjoy each other's company.

It had been her mother's desire while on her deathbed that she should be raised by her aunt, Annamma, so that she could learn to be a good housewife. So, around the age of ten, Annakutty was placed in her aunt's care. There was no doubt that her aunt loved her, but, due to her determination to raise Annakutty to be married to a wealthy and handsome man, she was a very strict taskmaster. Annakutty was transferred from her public school to another school by her aunt, and adjusting to the new school was difficult, especially given her aunt's rules that she was forbidden from talking to anyone there. While her aunt dressed Annakutty in the most fashionable clothing and expensive jewelry so that she might attract a husband, her classmates ridiculed her. Defying her aunt's attempts to adorn her, she would take the jewelry off on her way to school.

Contrary to her aunt's plans for marriage, Annakutty had plans of her own. The religious girl frequently prayed at the foot of the local Carmelites' altar, and, having gotten to know and develop a neighborly relationship with the order, she felt called to a religious vocation. Even at age twelve, she declared that, "Jesus is my only spouse and none other." The girl was determined.

Ignoring her call to religious life and with Annakutty only just barely a teenager, her aunt arranged a marriage for her thirteen-year-old niece, causing her to beg her uncle not to force her into it. She was so upset that she even fainted. Unfortunately, her aunt went ahead with her own plans and set a date for Annakutty's betrothal. Finally, an awful scene arose when she still refused to get married, and Annakutty took desperate measures. "What had

Betrothal: formal agreement to marry.

Saint Francis of Assisi: (1181/1182-1226) Born into a wealthy merchant family, as a young man Francis had a powerful conversion which led him to take on a life of holy poverty and live as a mendicant, begging for all he had. Called by God to repair the Church, he founded the Franciscan Order. He also received the stigmata. Today, there are countless orders of Franciscans.

Saint Clare of Assisi: (1195-1253) While still a teenager, Clare heard Saint Francis of Assisi's preaching and ran away from her disapproving family in order to join his way of life. The foundress of the Poor Clares, eventually her own mother, aunt, and sister joined her way of life. She was the first woman to write a monastic rule.

I to do to avoid it? I prayed all that night... then an idea came to me. If my body were a little disfigured, no one would want me!...O, how I suffered! I offered all for my great intention [to become a religious]."

Annakutty then took a drastic step. Since it was right after the time of the rice harvest, she sought out the pit where the chaff and husk of the rice grain were being incinerated. She had decided to burn her foot a bit to prove to her family and potential suitor, as well as his family, that she refused to be married and was instead called by God to the religious life. It was an extreme decision in a difficult situation, and not one that she made lightly, as she believed it was the only way she could prove her vocation to her family.

Unfortunately her ordeal only got worse. Instead of slightly burning her foot on the embers, Annakutty slipped and accidentally fell into the hot pit. She ended up with devastatingly grave burns on both legs, and

Ineffable: too great or extreme to be expressed or described in words.

her toes were so terribly burned and stuck together that doctors had to forcibly separate them, bandaging each one individually. During her time of healing from the burns, her aunt ceased her plan to forcibly marry Annakutty off. Even though it took almost a year for her legs to heal, their cure was total, so much so that the Vatican recognized the miracle.

Think of a difficult, or even painful, situation you have encountered in your life thus far. How did you handle it? Are you proud of the way it was dealt with? Why or why not?

It was around this time that she decided to join the Franciscan Clarist Congregation and follow in the footsteps of Saint Francis and Saint Clare of Assisi, another saint who had an amazing calling from God to give wholly of herself while still in her teens. At age seventeen, she became a postulant with the order on the feast of Saint Alphonsus Liguori, August 2, 1928, taking the name Alphonsa of the Immaculate Conception.

Franciscan Clarist Congregation: The Franciscan Clarist Congregation was founded in the late nineteenth century in India to carry out the mission of Saint Francis of Assisi. This religious community is rooted in a "spirit of prayer, life of hard work, care of the destitute and service of the poor, teaching of religion, and imparting education." Today, Franciscan Clarist communities can be found all over the world, praying and working according to the motto, "To holiness through lowliness."

But her aunt's pressure to marry didn't end there, as, during her year of postulancy, she even got the Franciscan Clarists' mistress of formation, the nun in charge of teaching the girls contemplating and discerning entering fully into religious life with the order, to agree that she could be married. But marriage was not in her future. At age nineteen, she, according to the customs of her order, donned a wedding dress and made her vows to the community; she then traded the wedding dress for a shaved head and the order's brown Franciscan habit on May 19, 1930. "I joined the convent to become a saint," Alphonsa said, "and having survived many obstacles, what have I to live for if I don't become a saint?"

Her new life in the convent soon revealed the extreme physical and emotional suffering she was to experience for the rest of her short life. A few months after receiving the habit, she had to be hospitalized and undergo surgery for rampant bleeding. Even as Alphonsa struggled with the pain, she experienced the added suffering of the other sisters even accusing her of faking illness to get attention.

Like the sisters' accusations that Saint Alphonsa was faking being ill to get attention, have you ever been falsely accused of something? What did you do to assert your innocence? How did the situation resolve itself?

Her health deteriorated, and the young postulant died July 7, 1946. In contrast to the crowds of people who now visit her shrine, few people, except for other Clarist Franciscans and the schoolchildren, attended her funeral. The veneration of Alphonsa and her grave started with the schoolchildren who, in life, she had always been kind to, but the beginning steps of the canonization process started December 2, 1953—only seven years after she died. Christians, Hindus, and Muslims have been healed through her intercession.

Her body was exhumed on April 13, 1957, and she was declared venerable on November 9, 1984. When she was declared a saint by Pope Benedict XVI on October 18, 2008, in Saint Peter's Square, Rome, ten thousand people came from India to honor their first national saint, with even some of her own family members in attendance.

What things in your life are keeping you from burning with love for God?

Chances are, when you think "Catholic," your mind immediately pictures Roman Catholic churches and the Latin rite Mass. The vast majority of Catholics in the world are considered Latin rite (or Roman) Catholics, however there are also many Eastern Catholic churches. The word "catholic" means universal, and these different and yet fully Catholic churches make this clear for us today. Catholics who worship in these communities celebrate the sacraments and are in full communion with the pope and the teachings of the Church, all the while celebrating the liturgy in many different ways. These churches have rich and beautiful heritages of faith, and learning about them can only strengthen our own practice of the Catholic faith.

Saint Alphonsa's parents were Syrian Christians, members of the Syro-Malabar Catholic Church. After Jesus' death on the cross, resurrection, and ascension into heaven, the apostles were filled with the Holy Spirit and on fire to tell of the Good News, the Gospel. Different apostles traveled to various places converting both Jews and gentiles alike to faith in Christ. One of these apostles was Thomas, that doubter we are all so familiar with who insisted in the Gospel of John that he would not believe that Christ had truly risen from the dead until he was able to see and touch the wounds in his hands and side. When he finally saw Jesus and was invited by him to "put your finger here and see my hands, and bring your hand and put it into my side, and do not be unbelieving, but believe," we can be assured that Saint Thomas' faith went even beyond declaring, "My Lord and my God!" Oral tradi-

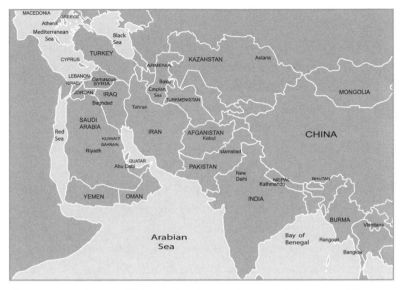

tion asserts this, and history backs up the rest of the story. Thomas traveled across the world to share this good news!

Saint Thomas the Apostle, doubter extraordinaire no longer, traveled to spread the Gospel in India. He preached on the Island of Socotra, going from there to Malabar, and from Malabar to Mylapore, and was martyred and buried in Mylapore. We know from ancient accounts in Edessa, which is located in modern-day Turkey, that his body was later moved there.

As the ancient Indian Christians, or Saint Thomas Christians, as they are called, relied on an oral relaying of history, there is no written telling of their Christian communities from the time of Saint Thomas to the arrival of the Portuguese in the fifteenth century during the European Age of Exploration. They were largely geographically isolated from the rest of the Christian world. That being said, the Syro-Malabar Catholics, Saint Alphonsa's family having been some of them, are descendents of those first Christians who were preached to directly from the mouth of Saint Thomas himself. And they are part of our Church today.

THE PRAYER OF SAINT ALPHONSA

Oh my Jesus, hide me in the wound of Your Sacred Heart.
Free me from my evil desire to be loved and esteemed.
Guard me from the mean pursuit of honor and fame.
Make me humble till I become a small spark
in the flame of love in Your Sacred Heart.
Grant me the grace to forget myself and all worldly things.
My Jesus, who is ineffable sweetness,
transform all the worldly consolations into bitterness for me.
Oh my Jesus, Sun of Righteousness,
enlighten my intellect and mind with your sacred rays.
Purify my heart, consume me with burning love for you,
and make me one with you. By Your Divine rays,
clarify my thoughts, illumine my mind, cleanse my heart,
consume me in the fire of Your love,
and thus unite me with You. Amen.

MEMORY VERSE
JOHN 20:28

Thomas answered and said to him,
"My Lord and my God!"

How did Saint Alphonsa echo Saint Thomas' words: "My Lord and my God!?" Give some examples from her life. Then, give some examples from your own.

Saintly Challenges

- Find out if there are any Catholic Churches in your area that follow an Eastern Rite, such as a Syro-Malabar Church. Consider attending liturgy here, or visiting the church for a tour and to learn more about this community in your area.

- Spend some time in front of the Blessed Sacrament discerning how God may be calling you to chastity in your own life.

    Remember that we live in a noisy world, and so silence takes practice!

- Put aside a chunk of your day for *Lectio Divina* (Divine Reading; see page 130). The story of doubting Thomas in John 20 is a great place to start, but also consider the *Lectionary* readings for the day or your own favorite passage.

- It's not necessary to only celebrate Saint Alphonsa's role as the first Indian saint in the July heat of her feast day! For a warm, yummy drink with hints of India, where Chai originated and is still a very popular recipe, drink to Saint Alphonsa's holy life! Enjoy making this recipe (found on page 129) from Bible foods cook Rita Heikenfeld (abouteating.com). The cloves and kick of cardamom are the perfect accompaniment to a good read.

JOURNAL YOUR THOUGHTS

BLESSED PEDRO CALUNGSOD

HE PLEASED GOD AND
WAS LOVED BY HIM

"Young friends, do not hesitate
to follow the example of Pedro,
who 'pleased God and was loved by him'
(Wisdom 4:10) and who, having come to
perfection in so short a time, lived a full life."

POPE JOHN PAUL II, MARCH 5, 2000, BEATIFICATION HOMILY

FEAST DAY: APRIL 2

PATRONAGES: YOUTH, THE PHILIPPINES, GUAM, ALTAR SERVERS

ur story doesn't start with Blessed Pedro, but instead his mentor, Father Diego Luis de San Vitores. Born on November 12, 1627, in Burgos, Spain, Father Diego joined the Society of Jesus, the Jesuits, in 1640. It was June 1662, at the age of thirty-four, when his life really got interesting. Sailing from Acapulco, Mexico, to the Philippines, his Spanish ship stopped on the island of Guam to restock food and water provisions for the one thousand five hundred miles left on their

journey. At that time, Guam was known as one of the Ladrones Islands, a name given it by the Portuguese-born Ferdinand Magellan and meaning "thieves." Even though they hadn't even hit land but had anchored off the shore of the island, Father Diego became totally struck by his short encounter with the Ladrones.

Blessed Diego Luis de San Vitores: The assassination of Padre San Vitores in 1672 by Matapang and Hurao.

On July 10, 1662, he arrived in the Philippines, an archipelago made up of seven thousand one hundred seven islands and islets, as a missionary. About five hundred miles off the southeast coast of Asia, the country comprises three major regions: the north is known as Luzon, the middle is made up of Visayas, and to the south is Mindanao. Even with the exploration of his new surroundings and much to do in the Philippines, Father Diego was enthused with the idea of going back to the Ladrones to start a mission. He petitioned the Philippine city of Manila's royal ministers but was told there was no ship at his disposal, no budget to pay for the costs of a mission, and no available priests to send. With such a negative response, Father Diego decided on a different tactic, skipped the middleman, and asked King Philip IV of Spain himself for his mission needs. King Philip responded with a "yes," issuing a ship named the San Diego for both the governor-general who procured the vessel on the king's behalf, as well as Father Diego himself.

Missionary: Jesus passed on his mission of spreading the Gospel to the apostles and commanded them to "make disciples of all nations, baptizing them in the name of the Father and of the Son and of the holy Spirit, teaching them to observe all that I have commanded you" (Matthew 28:19–20). Christians have lived out this call to spread the Gospel in many different ways throughout the centuries. The term *missionary* here refers specifically to the first evangelization, or preaching of the Good News, to those in non-Christian parts of the world. During much of the Age of Exploration, this type of missionary activity became very popular, as courageous explorers burned with zeal to share the Christian faith with those who had never heard of Christ before. Read sections 849–856 of the catechism to learn more about what we believe as Catholics about the Church's missionary activity.

Unfortunately, Father Diego was still not ready to set sail. He needed money to pay for the needs associated with the trip, as well as missionary manpower, hoping Jesuit Father Tomas de Cardenoso and fifteen or twenty Filipino Christian men to accompany him. They would need to travel halfway around the world, to Acapulco, New Spain (Mexico) to request the money for their religious mission, before they could proceed to the Ladrones. On August 7, 1667, the *San Diego* left the Philippines for Acapulco, with Father Diego Luis de San Vitores and Father Tomas de Cardenoso; some interpreters for the mission; and young lay assistants of about twelve to fifteen years old who worked with the Jesuits but were not in any formal way Jesuits themselves.

Among these young assistants was Pedro Calungsod. By the time Pedro had been born, Augustinians, Franciscans, Jesuits, and Dominicans had missions in the Philippines, but it is probable that his Catholic upbringing was deeply influenced by the Society of Jesus, whose members are known as Jesuits. The best proof that Pedro was a baptized Christian can be seen through his first name, which is a Christian name and that of the Church's first pope, Peter. His last name means "one's townmate," and while it is not clear when and where he and Father Diego first met, it must have been somewhere away from Pedro's hometown. We have no idea what he looked like except that he was a native of the Philippines from the Visayan region, whose people had a reputation as exceptional swimmers. He was possibly stocky, on the taller side, with tan skin, dark hair and eyes, and, since he was young, longer hair. He probably wore a shirt and long, knee-length shorts. Those who knew him described him as having a courageous and animated personality.

Imagine that you, like Blessed Pedro Calungsod, have been called to serve in a foreign land. Where in the world would you like to go? Why?

Carrying an image of Our Lady of Good Voyage, it took five months to sail from the Philippines to Acapulco, New Spain, now better known as Mexico, to ask for money from the government there. Days on board included daily Mass and sometimes violent storms. They finally arrived in Acapulco on January 6, 1668. Father Diego traveled to Mexico City to beg for the needed funds for his Ladrones mission, because at that point in time, officials there governed the Philippines. He was denied a number of times, until Mexico City was hit by an earthquake and the money was somehow found and allocated for the mission. In addition, private citizens gave articles such as clothing and furniture for the mission.

Our Lady of Good Voyage.

On March 23, 1668, they left

Acapulco on the *San Diego* for the Ladrones, bringing with them four additional Jesuits for the mission. They spent the time aboard the ship learning the Ladrones' Chamorro language, with Padre Diego also working on a version of a catechism in the native language. On Friday, June 15, 1668, land was sighted. It was Guam, the biggest and most southern of the Ladrones Islands.

At this time, on the island of Guam alone, there were twelve thousand islanders, while in the Ladrones as a whole, there were around thirty thousand. Chamorro men and women wore very little clothing and the men wore their hair totally shaved, except for the equivalent of a ponytail of hair on top.

The native people maneuvered their boats up to trade with the *San Diego* and were surprised when, instead of the crew simply attempting to trade goods with them, they called for them to come aboard the vessel. Taken aback, they hung back in their own boats until those aboard the San Diego began chanting the Litany of the Blessed Virgin Mary and Father Diego started preaching to them in their native language of Chamorro. One of those to come aboard was a man named Pedro, a Christian who had been shipwrecked on the island in 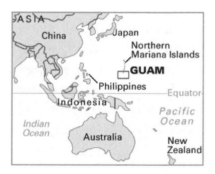 1638. He climbed onboard with his two-year-old daughter, Mariana, to have her baptized. As someone who, in the intervening years since the shipwreck, had become accepted by the people of the Ladrones, Pedro would turn out to be a valuable intermediary between the missionaries and the Ladrones people.

The Jesuits went to the chiefs of a village in the area known as Agana to negotiate regarding the mission they wished to erect. The very next day, they began to move themselves and all the articles they

Saint Ignatius of Loyola: (1491–1556) Born to a Spanish noble family, Ignatius became a priest and theologian and most famously founded the Society of Jesus, or Jesuits. Active during the period of Church history known as the Counter-Reformation, Ignatius and the Jesuits were known for their support of the pope and of Church authority, but their influence reaches far beyond their impact centuries ago. Ignatius was a mystic, and you may be familiar with his rigorous "Spiritual Exercises," a set of prayers and reflections that emphasize discovering the presence of Jesus in one's life and following him. In addition, Jesuits today are found in many different areas of ministry, but perhaps most visibly in education.

brought along with them off of the *San Diego* and started Mariana Mission. So on Tuesday, June 19, 1668, the *San Diego* left the island of Guam and its new missionaries and missionary assistants en route for the Philippines.

Padre Diego had an influence on what the so-called Ladrones would now be called by the European world. No longer would they be known negatively for their alleged thievery in the 1500s. Father Diego proposed "las islas Marianas," named for the Virgin Mary and the queen of France, whose royal support had made it possible long before most others thought it so. He also called each individual island by the name of a saint; for instance, Guam was known as San Juan Bautista, Spanish for Saint John the Baptist. While the saint names for the islands did not stick, they are still, even to this day, known as the Marianas.

The people seemed welcoming, so, in Agana, Guam, Father Diego's missionaries built a church and mission house, where they could spend time in prayer and other religious observances. They called this mission San Ignacio, dedicated to the Jesuit Saint Ignatius of Loyola. Before agreeing to baptize the Chamorro people,

Father Diego instructed them in the Faith, no doubt implementing the catechism he had formulated aboard ship. The missionaries and their assistants assembled the Chamorros, chanting the Act of Contrition and catechetical lessons in Chamorro, gave rewards to the pupils for their knowledge of the Faith, and would create a joyful, merry atmosphere of singing and dancing—another means of gathering the people together. In return, the people had to turn away from their idols.

Father Diego insisted that the men on the mission, both young and old, live Christian lifestyles, so as not to appear as hypocrites to the people they were preaching to. In regard to these standards, Pedro Calungsod, remembered by those who served the mission with him as being a "virtuous catechist," has been referred to as a longtime companion and a *"buen hijo"* (good son) of Father Diego. His duties included baptizing in an emergency when the Jesuits were not available and working as Father Diego's personal assistant, especially as the priest was extremely near-sighted and had to have a companion go ahead of him, leading by a rope tied to Father Diego's belt.

Dangers lurked on the island for the missionaries to the islas Marianas. They weren't traveling along the flattest of roads, and journeying by boat to other islands could also be treacherous. Additionally, they risked their lives by working for peace among warring Chamorro tribes. In the midst of such dangers, one much more lethal was lurking.

Choco, a Chinese man who was cast away into the Marianas while sailing from the Philippines to Indonesia, lived on Guam and purported to be a type of holy man dealing in sorcery. He viewed the Jesuits as competition for his spiritual notoriety, spreading rumors about them and saying that their baptismal water was poisonous. While there were those who continued to follow the Jesuits' catechesis, people began to turn away from the sacrament of baptism, and some of those who had already been baptized renounced the Faith.

Later, Choco himself turned back on the lies he had previously spread and became a catechuman and was subsequently baptized. During his baptism, however, two of Father Diego's Filipino assistants became demonically possessed. One ran away to the hill country and another began trying to stab Father Diego, and failing, stabbed one of their Christian companions repeatedly in the arm. Father Diego explained to the crowd that the devil had caused a scene to frighten them. It wasn't long after this before Choco had turned back to his old ways of sorcery and renounced his baptism.

Others of Father Diego's assistants also turned away from the Faith, going to live in community with Chamorros who had been baptized but fell away from the Christian teachings. Father Diego wrote to them with the love and mercy of Christ, offering them forgiveness through God the Father, and many came back to the mission. From testimonial writings we know that Blessed Pedro clung to his faith until his death, and this could not have been easy, especially in light of the evident struggles his companions faced in remaining steadfast to the mission.

What has kept you devoted to the Faith, even when those around you are having doubts or even falling away?

Apart from the conniving Choco, others opposed the missionaries' work on the island. The Macajnas, Chamorro holy men who dealt in magic, had widespread control over the people, who believed that they could control almost every aspect of daily lives. They, as well as Hurao, a village chief in Agana, saw the missionaries as a threat to their hold over the people. The Urritaos, young men who lived together unchastely with women who weren't their wives, also were wary of the Catholic missionaries, as Father Diego and his band were, of course, opposed to such behavior.

These groups were swayed by the Macajnas' encouragement to

bully the missionaries and so from September 11 to October 21, 1671, Hurao and a band of about two thousand went to battle against the missionaries. Fortunately for the missionaries, Father Diego, anticipating confusion, had prepared defenses in the way of fortifications. The Chamorros fought with lances that had burning tips, trying to set the mission's buildings on fire, but the missionaries prayed for rain. When their appeal was answered, the Chamorros were stunned, but continued to gather until the missionaries came out into the open to defend themselves.

After the fighting was over, Father Diego was aware that the mission was not completely in the clear, and yet he continued with renewed vigor in the mission's works. Early in 1672, he began preparations for four new churches to be built across the island of Guam, taking on the most difficult assignment, Nisihan, for himself. Along with a group of assistants that included Pedro Calungsod, he spent his time there building the church and catechizing the area's inhabitants, who were known for their rejection of the Gospel.

It was dangerous work. On Thursday, March 31, 1672, a young Mexican man who, like Pedro, was a missionary assistant, was killed in the process of sending a message from the main mission of San Ignacio in Agana to where Father Diego was stationed in Nisihan. There was also an attempt to start a fire at San Ignacio. After these incidents, Father Diego had all the assistants except for Pedro go back to San Ignacio for safety. He and Pedro made their way back in a more circuitous fashion, planning on looking in on some fallen-away Christians and continuing their catechesis and baptisms along the way.

By the time they were only seven miles from the mission at San Igna-

> **Catechize:** To catechize is "to reveal in the person of Christ the whole of God's eternal design reaching fulfillment in that Person. It is to seek to understand the meaning of Christ's actions and words and of the signs worked by him." CCC 426

cio, they heard that Matapang, who had been baptized after Father Diego had prayed over him and provided medical care for a lance wound, had recently had a new daughter. Father Diego and Pedro headed for his house to offer the sacrament of baptism to Matapang for the child. Perhaps swayed by those who had been working against the missionaries, Matapang responded angrily and irrationally. "I don't want you to baptize my baby because baptism is of no use!" he shouted. "Go away, you liar, or I'll kill you!" In his usual calm way, Father Diego replied that he simply wanted to baptize Matapang's child—and that he could kill him afterward, if he wished. As Matapang continued to refuse, Father Diego went out into the village and began to catechize the people. Matapang became further enraged at this. "I am sick and tired of your doctrines! I do not want to know more about God because he is evil and I hate him!"

Matapang began trying to gather a gang to murder Father Diego, and asked Hurao, who had led the battle against the missionaries earlier, to help him. Hurao was not immediately convinced that this was a good plan, reminding Matapang that the whole reason he was even still alive was because Father Diego had saved him. Hurao finally gave in when Matapang called him a coward, and he agreed to help Matapang kill the missionaries.

Meanwhile, Father Diego and Pedro Calungsod had baptized Matapang's baby. Instead of Father Diego, the first person to meet Matapang's fury was Pedro, who was rewarded for his faithful missionary work with spears. However, it wasn't so easy for Matapang to strike Pedro. Apparently, Pedro was quick and able to avoid the spears for a little while, as witnesses to the martyrdom commented on the ease with which he evaded the first spears that sought to end his life. Missionary assistants like Pedro weren't allowed to have weapons, otherwise, some thought he could have taken on the attackers. Instead, he bravely stood on the defensive. He neither ran nor tried to snatch up a weapon, working hard to dodge the attacks.

Finally, a lance plowed into his chest. Father Diego held the crucifix up in front of Pedro and gave him last rites before a sword wielder brutally chopped into Pedro's head.

Holding the crucifix he had just blessed Pedro with, Father Diego started preaching the Gospel to his assailants. Shortly thereafter, at 8 in the morning, Father Diego was also speared with a lance in the chest and had his head split into with a catana. With a rock, Matapang destroyed the crucifix Father Diego had carried. The men then stripped the bodies of Pedro and Father Diego of their clothes, dragged them to land's end, weighted their feet down with rocks, put them in a boat, and headed out to throw their bodies over the side of the boat. Soon, violent wind and lightning swept the area.

Accounts of Pedro's valor were passed around and recorded in art and other artifacts in his island community. These have been passed on to us and make it possible, though much time has elapsed, for the Church to never forget the sacrifice of a martyred priest and his young companion. When preparations for Father Diego's beatification were made in the 1980s, there was a renewed interest in the courageous story of his faithful assistant. Pedro was beatified on March 5, 2000, more than three hundred years after he was martyred.

PRAYER FOR THE INTERCESSION OF BLESSED PEDRO CALUNGSOD,

student, catechist, young migrant,
missionary, faithful friend, martyr,
you inspire us
by your fidelity in times of adversity;
by your courage in teaching the Faith
in the midst of hostility;
and by your love in shedding your blood
for the sake of the Gospel.
Make our troubles your own
and intercede for us
before the throne of Mercy and Grace
so that,
as we experience the help of Heaven,
we may be encouraged to live
and proclaim the Gospel here on earth.
Amen.

MEMORY VERSE

MATTHEW 10:32

*"Everyone who acknowledges me before others I
will acknowledge before my heavenly Father."*

*How did you declare yourself for Christ today? This week? If you didn't,
what's the deal? Why not?*

Saintly Challenges

- One of Blessed Pedro's responsibilities as Father Diego's assistant was helping him with daily tasks that were made more difficult due to the priest's limited eyesight. Seek out a non-profit organization in your area that helps people with visual impairment and see what service opportunities they might offer you.

- Pedro served as a catechist to the people on his missions. Investigate what opportunities there are for you to get involved with catechesis at your parish or school. Perhaps the Sunday School or Parish School of Religion classes need an assistant. Or maybe there is an opportunity to begin a Bible study or faith-sharing group at your high school. The opportunities to "teach Christ" are endless!

- Pray The Litany of the Blessed Virgin Mary, the prayer chanted by Father Diego and his missionaries upon first greeting the people of the island of Guam.

- The Litany of the Blessed Virgin Mary is also known as the Litany of Loreto, as it was first recited and popularized in Loreto, Italy. It is the Western Church's only approved Marian litany. A classic of Catholic spirituality, the litany includes the many titles attributed to Mary. Consider doing some research about the titles you're unfamiliar with.

JOURNAL YOUR THOUGHTS

JOURNAL YOUR THOUGHTS

SAINT MARIA GORETTI

A VALIANT GIRL

Our saint was a valiant girl.
She knew, she understood,
and that is why she preferred to die."

POPE PIUS XII, APRIL 27, 1947,
BEATIFICATION OF SAINT MARIA GORETTI

FEAST DAY: JULY 6

PATRONAGES: YOUNG PEOPLE, RAPE VICTIMS

Maria Goretti was born October 16, 1890, to Luigi and Assunta. When she was still a little girl, they moved from their northern Italian town of Corinaldo to seek more temperate weather and fertile land. Selling the house and their field, they brought their few personal items and a little money and set off with close friends the Cimarelli family. After weeks traveling the two hundred-mile journey, their ox-drawn cart piled high, they found themselves wandering through the metropolis of Rome for two days. Soon enough, they heard of a Count Mazzoleni with land to lease in nearby Nettuno.

A boggy, humid area known for malaria outbreaks, it wasn't exactly the land of milk and honey that they had been seeking, but each family moved into its own house, seeing that there were two that were unoccupied. By the next day both families were signed up with Count Mazzoleni as sharecroppers.

Valiant: displaying valor or heroism

The farm had been abandoned for three years, and Luigi worked hard to make up for lost time, growing wheat and barley, and, in the process, generally wearing himself down. He developed a light fever but kept working until his coughing led to a week's convalescence. Before long, he was back to laboring to bring the crumbling farm back to life and in essence trying to do too much himself.

Luigi's rationale was that if he didn't hire anyone, he wouldn't have to split the farm's income with anyone else. However, by well into harvest time, he was behind. There had been dizzy spells, episodes of lying paralyzed on the ground, and labored breathing. As a result, Count Mazzoleni became upset with his lack of progress and

Convalescence: a period of recovery or recuperation after an illness.

sent a father-and-son team, Giovanni and Alessandro Serenelli, to work with Luigi.

Giovanni was a widower whose wife had died in a mental in-

Sharecroppers: It was common in Italy at the time for peasant farmers to lease farmland from a large landowner and work the land themselves, paying as part of their lease a "share" of the harvest. Maria's family would have owed Count Mazzoleni a certain portion of their harvest each year, and they would have faced problems and possible eviction if their land did not produce enough harvest on which to live.

stitution, and Alessandro was his youngest son. They were new to the region, from not far from the Goretti's own hometown of Corinaldo, and spoke the same Italian dialect and had regional customs in common. Giovanni and Alessandro put in their share of the farm labors, and Alessandro, initially quite pleasant, would play with the Goretti children. But Alessandro was a broken young man. At eighteen years old, Alessandro was still bitter that he had been passed around to various relatives after his mother's death. Luigi didn't have the money to pay the Serenellis, so they lived and worked with the Goretti family, splitting their share of the harvests.

Winter was a slow time on the farm, and while Giovanni drank

steadily, Alessandro started exhibiting more and more loner behavior. He was known for being quiet, but seemed troubled on some level that nobody was able to articulate. He avoided social events, skipped Mass, and bought pornographic magazines by the stack, then staying locked in his room all day, cutting out the images and hanging them all around his bed. Assunta knew about his behavior but felt like she would be out of line to get involved, so she simply did her best to keep her children from entering the room. To make things more miserable for the Goretti family, Giovanni stole grain, and when Luigi tried to intervene and make sure each had his fair share, their relationship became more strained.

Sometimes family life gets stressful. What are some ways to handle this stress and support your parents in their vocation?

Luigi's health never fully recovered. He was suffering from malaria and by the end of April was on bed rest. Becoming progressively worse, he had difficulty breathing and was periodically losing consciousness. Finally, he asked for a priest to come to offer him the sacrament of the anointing of the sick and to usher him out of this life. Luigi's dying words were begging his wife to go back to their former home of Corinaldo.

While Assunta, a young widow, wanted to head back to her homeland, she didn't have the money or help to make it happen. Her children were still young, and so Assunta took her husband's place on the farm, and Maria took Assunta's place taking care of the household duties of cleaning, cooking, sewing, and generally caring for the needs of the other five children. According to her neighbor, Theresa Cimarelli, Maria "was a serious girl. She came and went quickly and busily" and "...was always modest and reserved," probably owing in part to the great responsibilities she carried at home.

Anointing of the sick: One of the seven sacraments, this is also known as the "sacrament of the dying" or "last rites." Administered by a priest, it involves prayers and the anointing with oil of the sick. This sacrament can be given to those who are sick or in danger of death because it brings to people the special grace of healing, comfort, and forgiveness of sins, helping to prepare them for death.

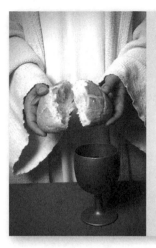

Feast of Corpus Christi: Also known as the Solemnity of the Most Holy Body and Blood of Christ, this celebration of the liturgical year is dedicated specifically to the Eucharist. It is most often celebrated by a eucharistic procession following Mass, in which a priest or bishop carries the monstrance displaying the Blessed Sacrament and the faithful follow in prayer and song. It is typically celebrated in the English-speaking Church on the Sunday following Trinity Sunday, during the Easter season.

On June 20, 1901, eleven-year-old Maria asked Assunta, "Mother, when will I make my first Communion? I can no longer live without Jesus." Assunta resisted. It was the custom at that time for children to not receive first Communion until age twelve. Maria's family didn't have the necessary money for the first Communion attire and were equally short on time and energy. In addition, Maria couldn't read or write, so how would she learn all that she would need to? Maria finally made her first Communion almost a year later on the feast of Corpus Christi. Various neighbors contributed different aspects of her outfit, and along with the fourteen other first communicants, she was encouraged in the homily to say three Hail Marys every night to venerate Jesus' mother.

Assunta reminded her, "You have received Jesus today. You must try ever so hard now to be good and pleasing to him," and try to please him she did. Every night, Maria said a rosary for her father, in addition to praying a Hail Mary when she passed his grave. The virtuous young woman valued purity, and so she was shocked when she heard a girl who has been in her first Communion class telling a vulgar joke at the town well. Her faith was an important part of her young life.

Do you remember making your first holy Communion? How did you feel? How do you approach the Eucharist differently today?

But Alessandro had developed an obsession with Maria. One day, Assunta was too exhausted to work with the men on the farm, and so Maria went instead. She was working side by side with Alessandro when he abruptly put down his hoe and began making sexual advances toward Maria, grabbing her arms. Repulsed, Maria broke free and ran away, hiding until lunch. Afterward, she managed to avoid Alessandro by stowing away into the hayloft, but it was difficult to avoid someone who lived in the same house. Days later when she was making the house's beds, he came up and grabbed her. She fought back by clawing him in the face, but when she went to tell her mother, Alessandro shook his clenched hand, warning, "If you say a word to your mother, I'll kill you." When she had hid in her room for too long to have lunch ready in time, Maria was reprimanded.

No one but Alessandro knew her private pain of living in fear of being near him. Maria began to follow Alessandro's vehement orders to her, knowing that she had to obey, risk the livelihood of her family, or be killed, and he continued to attempt to assault her, without success.

Alessandro became consumed with anger because Maria wouldn't return his affections, as well as increasingly fearful that Maria had told her mother about his advances, leading to further aggression on his part.

> **It is always OK** to seek help if you feel you are in danger of physical harm. There are many resources available for teens today that were not around during Maria's time. Talk to an adult you trust, such as a parent, teacher, or school counselor, if you ever feel threatened.

Without telling her mother why, Maria began to beg her mother to stay in the house. Time passed. Around lunch one day, Alessandro let Maria know he needed her to repair a shirt he had ripped, saying he needed it for Mass the next day. Maria sat at the top of the outside stairs to the house's second floor working on it and watching her baby sister, while everyone else was out in various areas of the farm.

But Alessandro had come up with a plan. He made an excuse, saying that he had to grab his bandana, and when he came in he headed upstairs to meet Maria where she was seated outside. Brashly, he ordered, "Maria, come here! Hear me! Come here immediately!" Seeing that he was about to seize her arm, Maria grabbed for the outdoor stairway's railing, but he was too strong for her and succeeded in pulling her into the locked farmhouse. Maria cried for him to let her go. He had a knife ready in case she resisted, and so she tried to shield herself using the table, but he threw it out of his way and heaved her down. Maria continued, "No! I will not, Alessandro, no!" It was 2 p.m. Maria told him he would go to hell if he did what he was intending, but he brutally stabbed her fourteen times. All the while, Maria tried to fend off his attack, until she ultimately passed out.

Alessandro thought that he had killed her, and so he cast off the knife nearby and barricaded himself in his room. Maria, nevertheless, managed to stand up and stumble to the front door, faintly calling for help before she fell unconscious again. Giovanni saw her and began yelling for Assunta, and when Assunta and the neighbors got to her, Maria's mother asked who had done such a thing and why. Maria answered, "Because he wanted to commit an awful sin, and I would not."

Domenico Cimarelli left for the doctor, telling neighbors along the route what had happened, and soon they began arriving with various weapons, with an aim at dealing with Alessandro themselves. They tried to force their way into his room, but Count Mazzoleni encouraged them to wait for the police, instead of taking the matter into their own hands. Alessandro didn't resist arrest, but instead lay motionless upon his bed.

It was around this time that the doctor determined that Maria needed an operation, and so they sent for a horse-drawn ambulance, which arrived around 6 p.m., four hours after her wounds had been inflicted. The chaplain visited Maria in the operating room, where the surgeon muttered to a priest, "Where you have found an angel, I am afraid we will leave but a corpse." The girl had damage to her intestines, lungs, heart, bones, chest, abdomen, and was suffering from internal bleeding. She then had to undergo two hours of surgery with no anesthetic, before she finally passed out, coming in and out of consciousness until 10 p.m., when she fell into a coma.

Saint Maria Goretti's commitment to purity is clear through the witness of her own life. Though many of us are not put in life or death circumstances such as hers, how can we follow her example and seek to live in purity and chastity, no matter the challenges the world throws at us?

The next morning, Maria received Communion, and the chaplain spoke to her of Jesus forgiving those who had put him to death, to which she thoughtfully replied, "Yes, for the love of Jesus I, too, pardon him, and I want him to be with me in heaven." Soon after, the police took down her statements on the attack and she explained to her mother why she didn't tell her earlier about Alessandro's harassing behavior, saying, "...he said he would kill me if I did. And you see, he killed me anyway." Maria received the sacrament of the anointing of the sick and died at 3 p.m. on July 6, 1902.

Picture someone who has wronged you and whom you have not forgiven? What will it take for you to get to that point? What is one concrete step that you can take toward forgiveness?

The entire town of Nettuno escorted Maria's body to the cemetery, but her mother did not stay on the farm long, moving back to Corinaldo with the rest of the family. Alessandro's father left the farm, as well, and Alessandro was moved from the jail in Nettuno to Rome. He countered that he had nothing to do with the accusations against him, before finally admitting his wrongdoing. Even so, he tried to plead insanity until it was ruled that he be punished with thirty years of hard labor, due to his being a minor, but still he seemed unshaken by his sentence.

But the story doesn't end here. Alessandro continued to fight against his own sense of guilt and against anyone who tried to free him from it—including a Catholic priest. He blamed the Church in which Maria had such strong faith for having "lost" her; if not for the teachings about chastity Maria learned as a young Catholic girl, he reasoned, she would not have resisted his advances.

But soon his heart would change and he would be able to see his own wrongdoing through Maria's intervention. While he was in prison, Alessandro reported that Maria appeared to him. "I saw her! I saw her! I saw Maria dressed in dazzling white, gathering beautiful white lilies in a garden and handing them to me," he said. "As I took them from her outstretched hands, they were transformed into small lights that glowed like candles." He immediately asked for a priest to come to him, and on November 10, 1910, he publicly repented.

His conversion of heart led him to write the following letter: "I am deeply sorry for what has happened. I have taken the life of an innocent girl whose one aim was to save her purity, shedding her blood rather than give in to my sinful desires. I publicly retract the evil I have done and beg pardon of God and of the stricken family. One hope encourages me—that I also may one day obtain God's pardon, as so many others have."

After he got out of jail, Alessandro continued to testify to Maria's innocence and her fight against him. On Christmas Eve 1937, the amazing occurred when Alessandro asked for Assunta's forgiveness and she granted it. "Maria forgave you, Alessandro, so how could I possibly refuse?" They went to church together on Christmas Day. He spent the rest of his life as a third-order Franciscan, working as a monastery gardener.

Maria Goretti was beatified on April 27, 1947, and not long after was canonized by Pope Pius XII, 48 years after her death, on June 24, 1950. Hers was the first outdoor canonization, and Assunta was the first mother to see her own daughter officially declared a saint. Alessandro was also present in the crowd, celebrating the faith of the girl whose life he had ended. A white marble shrine to Maria is in Saint Francis Church in her hometown, funded in part by Pope Pius XII and sculpted by Giovanni Scrivo. She is depicted prostrate with her arm uplifted in refusal, much like depictions of Saint Cecilia, and the bone of that arm is in the church's crypt chapel.

A shrine to Saint Maria Goretti.

PRAYER TO SAINT MARIA GORETTI

O beautiful and lovable Saint Maria Goretti,
Martyr on earth and now in heaven,
look down on us from your glory.
In your face we see the strength of your love
and your constant purity.
Through your life and death,
You bear the brilliant and victorious name of Christ.
We pray that we will be protected from all harm,
bodily and spiritual.
May we live with that same serenity of spirit, deep joy, and
commitment to purity to which you witnessed in your short life.
Amen.

—Adapted from Pope Pius XII canonization homily
for Saint Maria Goretti, June 24, 1950

MEMORY VERSE
MATTHEW 5:27–28

"You have heard that it was said, 'You shall not
commit adultery.' But I say to you, everyone who
looks at a woman with lust has already committed
adultery with her in his heart."

Do you think lust is more common today than it was in Jesus' time? Why
or why not?

What safeguards could you build into your spiritual life to help keep you
safe from impurity and lust?

Saintly Challenges

- Before logging on to the Internet, pray a quick prayer for help in using it for good and not evil, and especially for aid in avoiding impure imagery. Consider asking for the intercession of Saint Maria Goretti or Saint Dominic Savio.

- The next time you hear a peer telling a story or joke that is inappropriate, send the right message by calling him on it or walking away. Chances are, he was just telling it to fit in and will realize you don't appreciate it and think twice the next time.

- Saint Maria Goretti greatly missed her father after he died, making it a regular practice to pray a Hail Mary whenever she passed the cemetery where he was buried. The next time you pass a cemetery, pray a special Hail Mary for one of the people buried there, whether you were acquainted or not.

JOURNAL YOUR THOUGHTS

ADDITIONAL MATERIALS

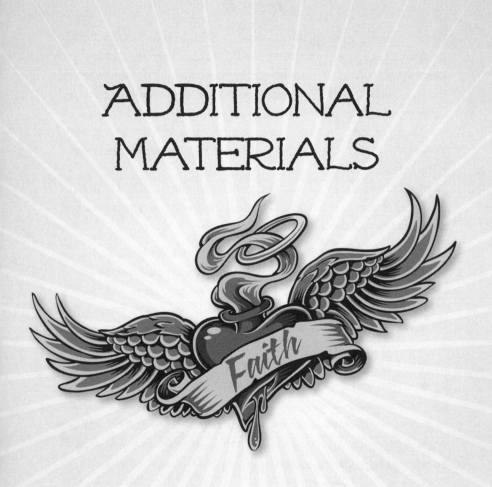

Death

During Dominic's time at the oratory, two of his best friends died of illnesses, which caused him grief and suffering, and reminded him that human life is fragile. Dominic always prepared for a holy death, whether through making confession and Mass regular events in his life, or by never letting an act pass by which could be undertaken immediately.

Once a month, Dominic went to confession and holy Communion as if it were to be his last. This exercise was known as the Exercise of a Happy Death.

Read the paragraphs from the Catechism of the Catholic Church on our beliefs about death below. How did Dominic's life reflect his deep understanding of these teachings?

1007 Death is the end of earthly life. Our lives are measured by time, in the course of which we change, grow old and, as with all living beings on earth, death seems like the normal end of life. That aspect of death lends urgency to our lives: remembering our mortality helps us realize that we have only a limited time in which to bring our lives to fulfillment: Remember your Creator in the days of your youth,...before the dust returns to the earth as it was, and the spirit returns to God who gave it.

How did Saint Dominic live in such a way as to remember his mortality? If you died tomorrow, would you have brought your life to fulfillment and be ready to be judged by God? Why or why not?

1009 Death is transformed by Christ. Jesus, the Son of God, also suffered the death that is part of the human condition. Yet, despite his anguish as he faced death, he accepted it in an act of complete and free submission to his Father's will. The obedience of Jesus has transformed the curse of death into a blessing.

Write down the names of family, friends, and acquaintances who have died. Pray for the repose of their souls tonight before you go to bed.

Poverty of Heart

Born into a family of privilege, when it came time for Juanita (Saint Teresa) to follow her calling into religious life, she chose a financially poor Carmelite monastery which was vastly different from the surroundings she had grown up around. Why would anyone follow such a radical call?

2544 Jesus enjoins his disciples to prefer him to everything and everyone, and bids them "renounce all that [they have]" for his sake and that of the Gospel.**335** Shortly before his passion he gave them the example of the poor widow of Jerusalem who, out of her poverty, gave all that she had to live on.**336** The precept of detachment from riches is obligatory for entrance into the kingdom of heaven.

How did Saint Teresa display detachment from riches in her own life? How can you better let go of material things for the sake of the Gospel?

2547 The Lord grieves over the rich, because they find their consolation in the abundance of goods.**341** "Let the proud seek and love earthly kingdoms, but blessed are the poor in spirit for theirs is the Kingdom of heaven."**342** Abandonment to the providence of the Father in heaven frees us from anxiety about tomorrow.**343** Trust in God is a preparation for the blessedness of the poor. They shall see God.

What kinds of "riches" do you have to work on becoming more detached from in order to enter the kingdom of heaven? How difficult is this for you?

Martyrdom

Kizito had only just been baptized a Christian when he was committed by the kabaka to be tortured and killed. He knew that, through baptism, he was entering not only into Christ's life, but also into a share of his death.

2473 Martyrdom is the supreme witness given to the truth of the Faith: it means bearing witness even unto death. The martyr bears witness to Christ who died and rose, to whom he is united by charity. He bears witness to the truth of the Faith and of Christian doctrine. He endures death through an act of fortitude..."

Saint Kizito knew that his baptism by Saint Charles Lwanga meant certain death, and yet, he heroically accepted the challenge. Would you have the courage to do the same amount of fighting for your own baptismal graces? Why or why not?

Euthanasia

By the end of her short life, Chiara was one sick girl. Her parents, however much they must have hated to see their daughter suffer, followed the moral law, as outlined in the catechism, until the natural conclusion of her life on earth.

2276 Those whose lives are diminished or weakened deserve special respect. Sick or handicapped persons should be helped to lead lives as normal as possible.

What does Chiara's witness at the end of her life teach us about the abilities of those who are sick or handicapped?

2277 Whatever its motives and means, direct euthanasia consists in putting an end to the lives of handicapped, sick, or dying persons. It is morally unacceptable.

Thus an act or omission which, of itself or by intention, causes death in order to eliminate suffering constitutes a murder gravely contrary to the dignity of the human person and to the respect due to the living God, his Creator. The error of judgment into which one can fall in good faith does not change the nature of this murderous act, which must always be forbidden and excluded.

Why is it wrong to end the life of a suffering person?

Legitimate Defense

Even though Stanislaus did not fight back in the face of his brother, Paul's, torment and physical abuse, the catechism tells us that self-defense when encountering an aggressor can be totally within the bounds of the moral law.

2264 Love toward oneself remains a fundamental principle of morality. Therefore it is legitimate to insist on respect for one's own right to life. Someone who defends his life is not guilty of murder even if he is forced to deal his aggressor a lethal blow:

If a man in self-defense uses more than necessary violence, it will be unlawful: whereas if he repels force with moderation, his defense will be lawful... Nor is it necessary for salvation that a man omit the act of moderate self-defense to avoid killing the other man, since one is bound to take more care of one's own life than of another's.

What type of use of self-defense in the face of an aggressor is not allowed?

Chastity

2348 All the baptized are called to chastity. The Christian has "put on Christ," the model for all chastity. All Christ's faithful are called to lead a chaste life in keeping with their particular states of life. At the moment of his baptism, the Christian is pledged to lead his affective life in chastity.

How did Alphonsa show a commitment to chastity?

Who is called to live out the virtue of chastity? How can you do this in your daily life?

Catechesis

God called Pedro to travel from the Philippines to live as a lay catechist serving with Jesuit Father Juan de San Vitores in Guam. This courageous mission to teach about Christ and his Church, which he never came home from, is his legacy, proving being young is no excuse for not spreading the Gospel and giving the greatest sacrifice and catechetical lesson of them all—the gift of one's self.

426 "At the heart of catechesis we find, in essence, a Person, the Person of Jesus of Nazareth, the only Son from the Father... who suffered and died for us and who now, after rising, is living with us forever."13 [...] Catechesis aims at putting "people...in communion ...with Jesus Christ: only he can lead us to the love of the Father in the Spirit and make us share in the life of the Holy Trinity."15

In your own words, what is catechesis? What is its purpose?

428 Whoever is called "to teach Christ" must first seek "the surpassing worth of knowing Christ Jesus"; he must suffer "the loss of all things..." in order to "gain Christ and be found in him," and "to know him and the power of his resurrection, and [to] share his sufferings, becoming like him in his death, that if possible [he] may attain the resurrection from the dead."17

How did Pedro "teach Christ" throughout his life? How did he teach Christ most powerfully?

429 From this loving knowledge of Christ springs the desire to proclaim him, to "evangelize," and to lead others to the "yes" of faith in Jesus Christ. But at the same time the need to know this faith better makes itself felt.

Pornography

Thinking back to the story of Dominic Savio, it took seriously heroic courage for Saint Dominic Savio to both resist the temptation of pornography himself, and also go the extra distance to pull it out of the grips of his schoolmates. It is known that Alessandro Serenelli, Maria Goretti's attacker, was addicted to pornography, and the catechism tells us exactly what it is and why it is so dangerous to our souls.

> **2354** Pornography consists in removing real or simulated sexual acts from the intimacy of the partners, in order to display them deliberately to third parties. It offends against chastity because it perverts the conjugal act, the intimate giving of spouses to each other. It does grave injury to the dignity of its participants (actors, vendors, the public), since each one becomes an object of base pleasure and illicit profit for others. It immerses all who are involved in the illusion of a fantasy world. It is a grave offense.

What types of situations and media put teenagers most at risk of the sinful and polluting effects of pornography?

How can you concretely guard your own mind, heart, and soul against pornography?

Cheese Empañadas with Onion (Makes 10 empañadas)

Dough:

> *2 cups flour*
>
> *1 stick butter (melted)*
>
> *1 tsp salt*
>
> *1 egg*
>
> *1 tbsp vinegar*
>
> *1/3 cup cold water*

Filling:

> *1¼ cup cheese (cheddar, Monterey Jack, Mozarella, or a combination)*
>
> *1 medium onion*
>
> *2 cloves garlic*
>
> *3 tbsp olive oil*

- Mix together flour, salt, and butter. In a separate bowl, mix egg, vinegar, and water. Once both have separately been blended, combine and continue to mix for five minutes. Chill dough for up to an hour.

- In the meantime, chop the garlic and onion, and sauteé until translucent. Shred the cheese and set aside.

- Once dough has chilled, make circular empañada pouches four to six inches across, and fill with cheese and onion mixture. Fold in half, and seal the pouch by pressing a fork around the edges. Fry in olive oil until golden brown, about three minutes. Remove empañadas from heat and place on a plate covered in paper towels. Allow to sit for two minutes.

Matoke (Serves 4)

4 plantains

2 tbsp lemon juice

1 tbsp butter

1 onion, finely chopped

1 whole chili pepper, seeded and chopped

½ bunch fresh cilantro leaves

2 cups vegetable or beef broth

Putting It All Together:

- Peel the plantains and slice into one-inch rounds. Cover them in water mixed with lemon juice, and set aside.

- Melt the butter on medium heat in a large saucepan. Fry the onions, chili pepper, and cilantro in the butter for three minutes.

- Drain the plantain slices. Add them to the saucepan and cover with vegetable or beef broth. Bring to a boil, then simmer over low heat for thirty to thirty-five minutes, until plantains are tender.

- Mash plantain mixture.

If you've never had a plantain before, imagine a banana that tastes like a potato. They are more starchy, less sweet, and can be dressed up for dessert or down for a main course. A truly international ingredient, plantains are also used in all kinds of cooking beyond East Africa and can most likely be found in your neighborhood grocery store.

Matt's Pesto

Since Chiara Luce grew up in the Liguria region of northwestern Italy, which, incidentally, is where pesto originates, this recipe is also appropriate for celebrating her feast day. This is one concoction that smells as awesome as it tastes, so put on your apron, get your olfactory glands cracking, and take a culinary journey to Chiara's homeland. Enjoy mixed into pasta (a little goes a long way) or in lieu of pizza sauce.

Ingredients

2 cups basil leaves

1/3 cup pine nuts

2 cloves garlic

1/2 tsp salt

1/4 tsp pepper

2/3 cup extra virgin olive oil

1/2 cup grated Parmesan

- Using a food processor or blender, grind the basil, pine nuts, garlic, salt, and pepper. Then, alternate grinding with pouring in the olive oil a little bit at a time. Using a spatula, transfer the mixture to a bowl and stir in the cheese.

Chai Tea

Ingredients:

5 tbsp cardamom pods

2 tbsp whole cloves

1 tbsp coriander seeds

6-8 cinnamon sticks, 2-inch long each

1/8-1/4 tsp black peppercorns

2 whole star anise

1 1/4 tsp ground ginger

- Combine all of the ingredients except the ginger in a non-stick ungreased heavy skillet. Over low to medium heat, toast the spices for about three minutes, until fragrant. Add the ginger and blend. Now you have to pound everything briefly, just enough to crush the spices coarsely. Some do this with a mortar and pestle, but you can also use a spice/coffee grinder, or put the spices in a plastic bag and pound with a mallet or rolling pin. Store in an airtight container for four months.

Brewing Chai Tea

- Combine 1 cup milk with about 2 tsp Chai mix and brown sugar or honey to taste (start with 1 tsp). You could also use a sugar substitute. Simmer and then turn off heat. Cover and let steep for 10 minutes while you brew a pot of Assam or Darjeeling (these are Indian teas—you could also use regular tea) using 2 cups boiling water and 2 tsp or 2 bags of tea. Reheat the spiced milk if necessary and strain into 2 large teacups. Pour in the hot tea and enjoy.

By sealing the ingredients into a bag and enclosing it with a copy of the recipe and a quote or prayer from Saint Alphonsa that powerfully strikes you, you can pass along a little taste of India and some seriously saintly wisdom to a friend or loved one.

Lectio Divina

Popularized by Saint Benedict in his Rule and traditionally practiced for an hour a day by monastics, *Lectio Divina* is the Latin term for Divine Reading.

Lectio (Reading)

* Read through the passage

Meditatio (Meditation)

* Slowly read the passage again
* Focus in on words that pop out at or really strike you
* if you'd like, write them down

Oratio (Prayer)

* Use the passage as a springboard for a conversation with God
* What does the reading have to say to you?
* Thank the Lord for this message
* What does the passage make you thankful for?
* Who does it remind you to pray for?
* What action(s) or change of direction is it calling you to in your life?

Contemplatio (Contemplation)

* Sit quietly, reflecting on what the passage has to say to you regarding God and his love
* No words are necessary

Sources

Bosco, John. *Life of Dominic Savio: Young Pupil at the Oratory of Saint Francis de Sales.* 6th ed. *Torino: Tipografia e libreria salesiana,* 1810. Originally translated by Father Wallace Cornell, SDB. Translation updated 2008 by Father Julian Fox, SDB.

John Paul II. Homily, pastoral visit to the parish of Saint Dominic Savio in Rome. December 7, 1997.

Catechism of the Catholic Church. 2nd Ed. Libreria Editrice Vaticana, 1997.

Compendium of the Catechism of the Catholic Church. Libreria Editrice Vaticana, 2005.

John Paul II. Angelus. Pastoral visit to Benin, Uganda, and Khartoum. February 17, 1993.

John Paul II. Address to the bishops of Uganda on their *ad Limina* visit. September 20, 2003.

John Paul II. Address to the ambassador of Uganda. March 21, 1980.

Benedict XVI. Angelus. Castel Gandolfo, Italy. September 26, 2010.

Zanzucchi, Michele. *Chiara Luce: A Life Lived to the Full.* Transl. Frank Johnson. London: New City Press, 2007.

Bodenschatz, Megan. "The word to Chiara Luce's peers." *Living City.* December 2010.

Kelly, Christine. "Ordinary, extraordinary life." *Living City.* March 2010.

Badano, Maria Teresa and Ruggero. "Chiara Luce." *Living City.* December 2010.

"Biographic profile of the Blessed Chiara Badano." Chiaralucebadano.it. March 31, 2010.

Community of Saint John. "Prayers." teresadelosandes.org. September 6, 2010.

Griffin, Michael D. *God, the Joy of My Life: A Biography of Saint Teresa of Jesus of the Andes.* Hubertus, WI: Teresian Charism Press, 1995.

John Paul II. Homily for the closing of World Youth Day. August 20, 2000.

John Paul II. Address of His Holiness John Paul II to the young people in Saint Peter's Basilica. November 15, 1978.

Coleridge, Edward Healy. *Quarterly Series: The Story of Saint Stanislaus Kostka.* Vol. 13. 2nd ed. London: Burnes & Oates, 1875.

Franciscan Clarist Congregation. "Saint Alphonsa". saintalphonsamma.org

Heikenfeld, Rita Nader. *Gifts Without Ribbons: Homemade Love.* Lakeside Park, KY: Rita Nader Heikenfeld, 2009.

Benedict XVI. "Homily for the Canonization of Four Blesseds." October 12, 2008.

Vatican News Service. "Alphonsa of the Immaculate Conception (1910-1946)." October 12, 2008.

John Paul II. "Beatification of Forty-Four Servants of God." March 5, 2000.

Leyson, Ildebrando Jesus Alino. *Pedro Calonsor Bisaya: Prospects of a Teenage Filipino.* Cebu City, Philippines: the Archdiocese of Cebu, 2000.

"Prayers." Blessed Pedro Calungsod, Lay Associates of the Missionary Oblates of Mary Immaculate.

Poage, C.P., Godfrey. *Saint Maria Goretti: In Garments All Red.* Tan Books and Publishers, 1998.